'*The Villain Edit* feels like an intimat
Alisha Aitken-Radburn shares her ex
ability—immensely relatable and readable!'

Yumiko Kadota, author of *Emotional Female*

'*The Villain Edit* is an unflinchingly honest look at the machine behind reality TV, and the way it intersects with the complexities of real life. A rare peek into how it feels to be hated by people you've never met, and subsequently loved by the same strangers. Ultimately *The Villain Edit* is a love story—one that's messy and raw, but far more meaningful than anything you can manufacture on TV.'

Clare Stephens, *Mamamia*

'Alisha's writing is self-aware, funny and captures both the universal and her unique experiences of womanhood in a zeitgeist committed to our shame and silence. *The Villain Edit* is relatable, deeply human and challenges the surface-level assumptions and stereotypes women in the public eye face. Reading this book felt like having a few red wines with a friend; there is deep comfort in Alisha's reflections and, as always, the truth is far more engrossing than the edit.'

Hannah Ferguson, *Cheek Media*

'A searingly, honest, intelligent and beautifully written book by a young woman who knows the inner workings of both political campaigning and reality TV. She reminds us powerfully of the feminist truth: the personal is political.'

Professor Catharine Lumby, author of *Frank Moorhouse: A Life*

'This book is real, honest and genuine, just like Alisha. She continues to challenge and change the narrative, and by writing this book she's chosen to rewrite her story and claim back her true self. I admire her for that, and I think she's courageous for doing so.'

Brooke Blurton, author of *Big Love*

'Eye-opening, heart-wrenching and jaw-dropping. This is as behind the scenes as it gets!'

Bridget Hustwaite, author of *How to Endo*

ALISHA AITKEN-RADBURN is a former Labor government staffer who appeared on both *The Bachelor* and *The Bachelor in Paradise*. She is a regular contributor to *Triple j*'s youth current affairs program, *Hack*, and the former host of *In the House and In the Senate*, featuring conversations with the women of Australian Parliament, and *Cocktails and Roses*, recapping *The Bachelor* and *The Bachelorette* with Osher Günsberg. *The Villain Edit* is her first book.

ALISHA AITKEN-RADBURN

THE VILLAIN EDIT

A memoir about reality TV and
taking control of the narrative

ALLEN&UNWIN
SYDNEY • MELBOURNE • AUCKLAND • LONDON

Some names and identifying details have been changed to protect the privacy of individuals.

First published in 2023

Copyright © Alisha Aitken-Radburn 2023

Allen & Unwin
Cammeraygal Country
83 Alexander Street
Crows Nest NSW 2065
Australia
Phone: (61 2) 8425 0100
Email: info@allenandunwin.com
Web: www.allenandunwin.com

Allen & Unwin acknowledges the Traditional Owners of the Country on which we live and work. We pay our respects to all Aboriginal and Torres Strait Islander Elders, past and present.

A catalogue record for this book is available from the National Library of Australia

ISBN 978 1 76106 885 0

Author photo by Renae Roberts
Set in 13.25/21 pt Garamond Premier Pro by Bookhouse, Sydney
Printed and bound in Australia by the Opus Group

10 9 8 7 6 5 4 3 2 1

MIX
Paper | Supporting responsible forestry
FSC® C001695

The paper in this book is FSC® certified. FSC® promotes environmentally responsible, socially beneficial and economically viable management of the world's forests.

Life is not a problem to be solved,
but a reality to be experienced.

For Mum, for giving me everything.
For Alex, for getting me through.
And for Glenn, for being my biggest fan.

CONTENTS

PROLOGUE

A Bad Person

'It's going to be okay,' the psychologist said. She said that my memories of filming the show would always be valid and always remain mine, no matter what made it to air. She was responding to yet another anxious phone call as the premiere date of season six of *The Bachelor* crept closer and closer.

This time, I'd called her from a Canberra hair salon. I was getting a fresh full head of foils. I had timed my salon visit perfectly: about two weeks out from airing, just enough time for it to fade a little if the blonde was too bright. I'd be ready for the masses of press interviews I thought awaited me. I would soon drive up to Sydney to stay with my best friend Hannah for six weeks so we could watch the episodes together at seven-thirty p.m. every Wednesday and Thursday night.

As the bleach developed, my conversation with Alex, the show's psychologist, weaved in and out of my insecurities. I hadn't struggled with opening up to a psychologist; in fact, I'd later learn that I was one of the participants who took most advantage of the free counselling, with Warner Brothers picking up the tab. Alex gave me all the reassurance you would hope to receive from a psychologist. She assured me that all the other girls would be feeling similar trepidation—after all, a very intense window of our lives was about to be broadcast to over half a million Australians. We had all gone through a very specific set of experiences together and those experiences would bond us, regardless of any TV narrative laid on top.

She told me that I would be fine. I had a strong support network of friends and family around me, and at the end of the day their opinions were the only ones that really mattered. With the wave of calm I'd been seeking washing over me, our conversation meandered to less loaded topics, like how fucking freezing Canberra was in July and how it was totally fine I'd resigned from my respected staffing job in Parliament House to do *The Bachelor* because who could spend another winter sitting in front of a tiny Kmart heater anyway.

But it wasn't going to be okay. A fortnight later, as the show began to air, the backlash began too.

It started benignly enough. I had developed a ritual of voraciously reading every little bit of commentary on *The Bachelor* after each episode aired. My dance began with *Bachelor Unpacked*, a comedic recap posted on *The Bachelor*'s Facebook page. The ten-minute recaps were pre-recorded by comedians Tanya Hennessy, Brianna Williams and Mat Whitehead. They would watch screener copies of the episodes—early drafts of the final edit that are ninety per cent of the way there. Because the recaps were pre-recorded, they were uploaded immediately after the episode.

Next I'd head to #TheBachelorAU hashtag on Twitter, then *The Bachelor* Instagram and then a collection of fan pages I was following from a throwaway Facebook account I'd set up specifically to lurk the groups.

The final and most important stop on my journey was an online forum for *Bachelor* superfans. These fans didn't just follow the Australian show. They dissected every iteration of the franchise they could get their hands on—from the flagship US version to *The Bachelor Ukraine*. And they didn't just watch it, they sleuthed each series. They'd hunt down paparazzi pictures to discover who the next set of *Bachelor* contestants might be, stalk their social media and hypothesise about when they'd be eliminated and why. There was regular speculation about the casting of the leads—who would be crowned the next Bachelor and Bachelorette—and when the seasons went to air there were designated threads for members to share their thoughts live as the episodes were broadcast.

I checked the forum so often that I came to recognise the forum regulars—such as GuardianAngel, Butterflylove, DirtyStreetPie and Bobette—and even to know their unique personalities, what characters they clicked with the most, what behaviour from contestants they despised, and their big-picture perspectives on the producers and the future of the show.

This strict ritual took about two hours and afterwards, finally satisfied that I'd consumed every piece of content available, I would drift off to sleep, knowing there was another episode to come.

By the time my elimination episode aired, this ritual had soured.

Ten-thirty p.m.

Alone in my bedroom, I began scouring the internet's reactions for the final time. The room filled with the soft glow from my phone as I scrolled through that night's verdict. Comments about my wit and charm had been replaced with hundreds of comments calling me ugly, a dog and quite consistently instructing me to get a nose job. Someone tagged their friend, writing 'She's not pretty enough to be that bitchy.' One called me a putrid rat. Another said, 'See ya later LAP DOG TURD.' Eloquently put.

Midnight.

I left Instagram, hoping for a reprieve on the forums. What did Bobette think of my elimination?

'The Axis of Evil is no longer.'

'The wicked witches are dead!!!'

No relief there.

I stared up at the intricate patterns in the plaster of my ceiling, taking stock of the damage. One comment was fixed in my mind. I would try to lead my thoughts to something unrelated, the next day's work or another TV show. I'd try to will myself to sleep, but the comment returned.

'You are a bad person.'

A bad person. It was the worst of them all. I could handle a lot, but this undid me. I rolled onto my side, staring into the curves of each letter on my screen until they flickered into a blurred mess. I knew I could do bad things. I could be selfish and unthinking. I could be arrogant and an asshole. My teens and twenties had been littered with mistakes and misjudgements, but I had always notched that up to being young, dumb and human. Not a bad person.

There was something so particularly scathing about that comment that it sent me spiralling in a way I hadn't the entire time the show had been airing. Australia had picked apart our appearance, our personalities, our mannerisms and our clothing. We had been scrutinised for who we sat with in a particular scene, our inflection as we read a date card, the hemline of our dress at a cocktail party, but this comment broke me.

Those five words completely shattered the image I'd built of myself in my mind. I thought I had a worthwhile personality. I thought I was someone people would like to know. I knew I wasn't a comedian but I thought I was funny. I thought I was kind but not so much that I was boring, or that it was laid on so thick that it seemed inauthentic. I thought I was an interesting person. I thought I was a good person. My reason for choosing to do the show had been, in part, to seek validation of that. But the audience had clearly disagreed. Here, with five simple words, my reality came crashing head-to-head with another.

My heart pounded.

Three a.m.

What the fuck have I done?

CHAPTER 1

The Application

I sat on the bed of my hotel room in Paris next to a half-drunk bottle of red wine and a half-eaten packet of prosciutto, wondering how to describe myself. How do you capture a full person in a couple of sentences on a web form?

Some of it was easy enough: my full name, date of birth and email address. Then there were some questions about what I looked like. How much did I weigh? What was my dress size? *What size was too big? Would I be put in the 'no' pile if I wrote a number too large?* I could oscillate from a size 8 to a size 12 and I was currently alone, overseas, after a pretty rough break-up, living on a diet of camembert and cabernet sauvignon. Nevertheless, I couldn't take any chances. I put an 8 in the box.

'Tell us about yourself in a sentence.'

Where could I possibly start and what should I include? They probably want to know what I'm like in a relationship. *Should I say that I'm recently single?* Maybe I'd include that I had really thought my last boyfriend would be my last, that I'd thought he was 'The One'. That would make me look serious about finding love.

Do I tell them that I'd thought I was about to nail my timeline? I'd set it in my first year of uni with my girlfriends over bottles of Passion Pop on that dirty second-hand couch pushed up against the outside laundry. Engaged at twenty-six. Married at twenty-eight. I'd just turned twenty-five, and while I was always up for a challenge, this last year had brought some tight reversals.

Do I tell them that I walked 20,000 steps around the various arrondissements and attractions of Paris yesterday, and all I could think the whole time was that my ex-boyfriend had been the pinnacle of compatibility for me in this life and now that it was over I would never meet anybody else ever again and end up dying alone? Do I tell them that I'd woken up this morning to find that last night I'd sent a direct message to American singer-songwriter Jewel saying *dude listsned to you wong just the loved it* and followed it two minutes later with *sorry I am very emotional and drunk*?

Jewel hadn't replied.

Maybe it was best to concentrate on personality traits. I typed 'optimistic, fun-loving, intelligent' into the text box. *Did that sound conceited?* I deleted intelligent and reached for my phone to message Hannah. We'd met at The University of Sydney through student politics and share-housed together for three years. We were inseparable, our lives a blur of nights that turned into mornings. Of The Rubens blasting from our iPhones because we refused to invest in a proper Bluetooth speaker. Of philosophical debates in our front yard, which despite our best intentions—and occasional googling of 'how to install turf'—was a mess of dirt and broken tiles, and weeds we'd grown attached to because they flowered in September. Hannah would know what I should write.

'How would you describe me?' I messaged.

Three dots blinked on the screen.

'Smart. Fun. Inquisitive. Captivating. Exciting,' she replied.

Her calling me smart made me feel like less of a dick about calling myself intelligent, and while I thought describing myself as captivating would be a bit much, I basked in the compliment regardless.

Should I mention my job?

That's usually the first thing people mention when someone asks them about themselves. We don't mingle at parties and ask people their name and then what brings them true happiness, or what defines them as a human being. We ask, 'What's your name and what do you do?' Then they reply with, 'I'm John, I'm an accountant,' or, 'I'm Sally, I'm a junior analyst,' and then our response sits somewhere on a spectrum of impressed to indifferent to 'What the fuck is a junior analyst?'

My job had definitely become a central component of my identity. I jumped at the chance to answer 'What do you do?' at a party.

I was working for Labor Opposition Leader Bill Shorten. In the last federal election, the Labor Party had been seven seats short of forming a majority government and now, two years later, in 2018, the office was gearing up to finally make Bill Shorten prime minister.

I was on his media advance team. The advance team, or 'advancers', would fly around the country a day or two ahead of Shorten, organising his events and appearances and making sure they ran smoothly and gaffe-free.

But it wasn't just the job in Parliament House that had become my identity. It was the Labor Party. I'd joined the Party in my second year of university, and soon enough my weekends were spent knocking on doors in marginal electorates asking people if they planned to vote for their local Labor candidate in the upcoming election—whether that was local, state or federal. My nights were often spent at Labor's Parramatta call centre canvassing voters in a different state, for a different election.

I hadn't noticed the extent to which the Labor Party had consumed my life until I was invited to a party with a group of friends that I used to go clubbing with, religiously, each Saturday night in Sydney's Kings Cross. A boy at the party, Angus, a former boarder at one of Sydney's most elite private boys' schools, had sidled up to me halfway through the night and said I was really into 'that Labor shit, hey?' He'd then made a gross joke about Julia Gillard and informed me the Labor Party wouldn't be elected for another decade after our 'dabble in female leadership'. These jabs from guys like Angus galvanised me even more. They just didn't get it and I felt like I'd discovered a community of people who did.

Life was so difficult for so many, and most people in power didn't understand that because they'd simply had no experience of it. They'd never had to worry about rent money or compare prices at the supermarket. They'd never had to ring up their electricity provider to get the lights turned back on. Problems like that had just never been part of their reality.

But in the Labor Party, I met people who understood. People who knew that life was hard and were passionate about making it easier, even just a little bit. For the first time, this family of people had given me a language to explain what I wanted to see happen in the world: social mobility, fairness, equity. When I first joined, I attended as many events as possible, listening to the speakers articulate what I had never been able to. I added their words to my lexicon and tried to emulate them where I could. And then, just six years later, I was working for one of them. I was proud to work for Bill Shorten and I was proud to be in the Labor Party.

I looked back at the box on my screen. Maybe my job would give me a little bit of an edge, some intrigue as they sifted through the applications. Amid accountants and junior analysts, it would definitely stand out. I took a couple of Hannah's nice adjectives, slotted in that I was a political staffer and ended the description with the fact I was 'looking for love'.

I looked at the sentence glowing up from the computer screen. I kind of hated it but didn't know what else to write. I'd spent twenty minutes on this answer alone. It would have to do. I took another swig of red wine directly from the bottle and scrolled down.

'Tell us about your parents. How old are they? Are they still married? If so, how long have they been married for?'

Christ.

The little window they'd provided to write in was definitely not big enough for this one.

My mum and dad were both in their fifties. They were not married, had never been married. My dad had not really been part of my life. I'd spent a handful of days with him over the years, until I'd turned eighteen and decided I deeply resented him for abandoning me. Since then, I'd seen him even less.

According to Mum, they met at the Astor Hotel in Goulburn on New Year's Eve in 1991. They went home together that night and then he followed up for a second date at the Goulburn Brewery the next week. Mum was living in Cairns at the time and only back home for the holidays, so their flirtations continued over the phone once she left. From Mum's account, the tryst was passionate, fun and casual.

That was, until the positive pregnancy test.

Not that being pregnant was necessarily a problem. In fact, Mum—thirty-two years old and a little lost about her next chapter in life—was pretty excited at the prospect of having a baby. But having a baby with a cute guy you had a one-night stand with definitely made things less casual.

Mum recalls calling him and sharing the news pretty bluntly. She received an equally blunt response. He had a wife. They lived in Canberra. They'd been married for ten years.

I had always thought it was a good story. I loved to bring it out at parties with strangers I'd just met. I loved to hear them exclaim 'No!' when I dropped that last bombshell. It was a fact that I'd carried my whole life, so I was relatively detached from it, and it felt like an easy trade: a deeply personal detail for an instantaneous connection.

Maybe I could do the same thing here? Maybe my little trauma token would be endearing to whomever was reading this application. I crafted the key points into something more succinct.

'When did you last cry and why?'

Thirty minutes ago. Just before I'd clicked on this link.

It was Christmas Day, and before I decided to spill my whole life into an application for *The Bachelor* I'd been aimlessly scrolling Snapchat. I had ended up clicking on five consecutive stories of people celebrating with their families back in Australia. All in colourful paper hats, all with charged glasses of champagne and tables laden with all Aussie favourites: endless plates of oysters, piles of prawns and tangy, pink cocktail sauce. Christmas was my favourite time of the year, and while I'd intended this solo jaunt to Europe to be the peak of my feminist empowerment, I had never felt more alone. I'd clicked on one more story. The ugliest-looking Christmas trifle I'd ever seen. I'd burst into tears.

Everyone was together. Everybody was with someone they loved. And here I was, surrounded by deli meat in a hotel room with *Eat Pray Love* playing in the background.

I'd been planning this trip for the past six months, except six months ago I'd been planning it with my boyfriend of a year and a half. The boyfriend I'd thought was The One. My soulmate, my romantic destiny and my ticket to happily ever after. That boyfriend was now an ex-boyfriend, which had left me with an itinerary stacked with the most romantic hotels in Europe. My mistake was not rebooking the lot. When I'd landed in London I should've gone straight to the most debaucherous hostel I could find. The type of hostel where if you buy a bucket of shots you get a free T-shirt that you'll inevitably spew on after you hook up with a guy from Melbourne even though you were looking for a cute British guy. But even the mediocre guy from Melbourne would've been a better option than getting straight onto the Eurostar and opening the door to a bed covered with rose petals at Hôtel Mademoiselle.

The elaborate European holiday was one of those classic manoeuvres where you make a big gesture to distract from fundamental issues in your relationship. Sometimes it's a ring, sometimes it's a puppy, sometimes it's a detailed itinerary traversing England, France and Italy.

About three weeks before embarking on the holiday, The One and I had been in yet another fight. We'd been doing long-distance between Sydney and Canberra and I'd come to Sydney for the weekend, thanks to work. One of my closest friends from uni, Jen, was having birthday drinks in Surry Hills. I hadn't seen Jen or the group of friends that would be at the party for what felt like years. The One told me that if I chose to go I wouldn't be prioritising our relationship—I was in Sydney and therefore it was his time. Every time I came to Sydney was his time. No friend time, no me time—just his time. And every time I tried to assert myself, calmly outlining why seeing my friends was important to me and why my independence mattered, he would lock me into hours of back-and-forth arguing via text or Facebook Messenger. The fights would envelop my workday and distract me to the point where nothing else could occupy my mind.

My Google search history was filled with 'Is [insert action here] degrading?' and 'Is [insert behaviour here] controlling?' The notes app on my iPhone had a list of words he'd called me in our fights. I was cataloguing them because whenever I found myself back in battle with him, he made me doubt my own memory of events. Slut. Heinous bitch. Lying bitch. Cunt.

The words were there on my phone, along with the time and date I'd written them down: 8.28 p.m., 19 April 2017. But even when I referenced the note directly, even when I cited the exact date and time, my reality was somehow overruled.

I'd already tried to end the relationship a couple of months earlier, but he'd become so upset that he'd had a nosebleed. I hadn't been able to do it. I had been so prepared, I'd listened to 'Flawless' by Beyonce about ten times on the flight to Sydney, yet I just hadn't been able to muster the strength. How do you break up with someone while their nose is bleeding?

But this particular fight was the straw that broke the camel's back. This time I was resolute. We were three hours deep into our routine of back-and-forth messaging in the middle of a workday and as usual it was like talking to a brick wall. I would express what he was doing to hurt me and the change that I needed to see in the relationship, and he'd twist the narrative until I was in the wrong. I would try to craft my sentences precisely, in the hope it would unlock some recognition in him.

I was so exasperated that I started crying at my desk.

My eyes remained focused on the computer and the conversation but tears were quietly rolling down my face, off my chin and onto the keyboard. The quiet tears eventually became gulps of air as I tried to moderate my breathing. Despite my best efforts, the sounds alerted my colleague Lex, who was at a desk nearby. She came over, parked herself next to me and listened as I recounted the whole situation.

It wasn't the first time she'd heard about one of our fights.

Stories of his overbearing nature had unfortunately become all too common in my friendship group. There was the time I'd just moved to Canberra for work and everyone had been gearing up to watch the third State of Origin game at a local bar political staffers frequented. It would be the first social event where I could get to meet new people and make new friends. I shared my excitement with him, and he told me I needed to watch the game at home on FaceTime with him.

There was the time we had tickets to a performance in Camperdown and he told me I needed to wear the same outfit I'd worn the previous year with my previous partner. I'd told him it made me feel uncomfortable. He'd told me he wouldn't come if I didn't.

There was the time we stood on Glebe Point Road after a romantic dinner and he yelled at me relentlessly about something I'd said. A passer-by intervened to ask if I was safe. I'd said I was and thanked them. He gave me the silent treatment once we were home.

Throughout this relationship, my messages to my friends were full of rationalisations of his behaviour, downplaying things I would only get the courage to tell them about after a few drinks.

Lex listened intently as I explained the latest in the saga. I told her I hadn't seen Jen since I'd moved to Canberra and that my boyfriend had told me that I was being selfish in planning to go to her drinks.

She looked at me and said, 'Alisha, if it wasn't for Europe, would you break up with him?'

'Fuck yes,' I replied, without hesitation.

'So, let's work that out then.'

It was one p.m., the middle of our workday, but Lex took me down to the bar below the Commonwealth Parliamentary Offices in Bligh Street, ordered a bottle of wine and helped me game plan. We wrote down every different element of the trip and who had paid for what: the connecting flights, the hotels and the wine tours. We worked out how much I'd have to pay him if I were to go alone and she helped me craft my final, determined messages. To the very end he argued with me, even about the time I'd meet him at a cafe to have the conversation.

The break-up was a relief.

My notes app had become my greatest confidant. I'd written lists of the awful things he'd done to remind me not to get back together with him and it sat above a list titled 'Things I can't do if I am with him again'.

'Buy a cute apartment in Canberra.'

'Get my lips done without feeling denigrated.'

'Read and study whenever I want without complaints.'

For months he had managed to twist our conversations into the ways I was mistreating him. For months I had felt on edge, trying to figure out whether there was actually merit in what he was saying. Maybe I was the problem. Maybe I was hurting him. I had completely lost my ability to trust my own thoughts and feelings.

I went to Jen's party that night and I went to Europe without him. I felt free.

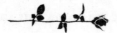

'Is there is anything you regret doing in your past relationships? What is it?'

Yes. Lots of things. Why were these answer boxes so small?

I had always projected the idea that I lived life with no regrets. Fast and loose, collecting stories to reminisce about with Hannah when we inevitably ended up drinking wine on the porch of our retirement village, hopefully having upgraded from Passion Pop by then. But the truth was I had endless regrets.

I sometimes felt like I was moving through life like a battering ram. I was undeniably collecting stories, but anyone involved in my anecdotes was collateral damage. I would revel in sharing tales about bad dates, terrible sex and dreadful ex-boyfriends that I should never have gone back to. The stories might have been a hit with whatever audience I was commanding but in the back of my mind was always the shameful awareness that I wasn't the only player in the production.

The most recent casualty of my selfish impulses had been Tom. Our relationship came just before I met The One. He was lovely. We lived on different sides of the country and flirted via Facebook comments until I booked a flight to go and meet him in Perth. There wasn't anything particularly wrong with our relationship, it just didn't feel like the love I was so desperately seeking. We were really good friends but I was looking for fireworks. I was looking for that explosive, rom-com lust, brimming with anxiety and tension, where any obstacles were overcome in the end simply through the power of love.

With The One, there was banter and anticipation. He made me feel wanted. We would go drinking 'as friends' while I was still dating Tom. We would chat late into the night, flirting and pushing boundaries, relishing the risk. Until one night, after far too many glasses of red wine in a bar I knew I definitely should not have been in, the emotional cheating morphed into physical. We kissed. I knew the moment our lips touched that I'd have to end it with Tom.

I had made a habit of this: I was never honest with myself about when a relationship had reached its emotional end and I never wanted to hurt the other person by telling them so. Instead of doing the right thing—being honest and telling my partner I wasn't happy—I would continually allow myself to be captured in the exciting first stages of something new, until I was blowing up the old relationship. In an attempt to spare someone's feelings, I would damage them more.

I booked a flight to Perth to break the news. Hannah queried whether it was really necessary to fly for over five hours to tell the poor guy that I'd kissed someone else but apparently my morality had re-emerged. I landed close to midnight the next day and got an Uber to his house. As unfamiliar city lights blurred past the car, I game planned the weekend. Maybe I'd hold off with the news until the morning? That would be the kind thing to do. By the time I'd reach his house it would be nearly one-thirty a.m. and it wouldn't be nice news to drop on someone half asleep.

He definitely wasn't half asleep. While I was game planning, my boyfriend was pre-gaming. We were uni students and at the peak of our 'let's go clubbing every night' phase. He greeted me with a shot of tequila, ready to hit Perth's Northbridge nightlife precinct. My guilty conscience couldn't wait until the morning.

I blurted out my secret on his front doorstep. 'I'm so sorry, I kissed someone else.'

His face fell. My heart fell.

He didn't say anything at first, just dropped his hand. The tequila fell sadly out of the shot glass, splashing onto the steps. We walked into his bedroom in silence, where we lay for the next four hours. The first hour we didn't talk. I wasn't there to explain myself. I knew I had done the wrong thing, the cowardly thing. I was there to be accountable. But he wasn't saying or doing anything. I had expected him to swear at me, punch a wall, scream in anger, but he was silent. As the night dragged into the early hours of the morning, he looked at me and said, 'We can work through this.' And, 'It's fine.' And, 'I forgive you.'

Except I didn't want to work through this. I wanted to break up. It was the reason I had thrown this grenade: to blow the whole thing up. It had been a cruel, shitty thing to do to somebody, but I wasn't courageous enough to have a direct conversation. I didn't know what to do. There we were, in his classic boyish bed—he had a bed frame and a fitted sheet, but not much more—lying together all night in awkward silence. I wished the bed would swallow me whole.

I shouldn't have done it on the first night. I still had over twenty-four hours in Perth. My bloody flight was at three p.m. on Sunday and it was now nine a.m. on Saturday. I asked him if he wanted me to leave. I had a handful of friends in Perth; they were mostly his, but they'd understand. I'd explain the situation and surely they'd let me crash on a couch. But he was decided: he didn't want me to leave, he wanted to work through it.

Twenty-four hours of working through it. Isn't it funny how much the speed of an hour is relative? An hour at after-work drinks disappears in the blink of an eye. An hour at the gym drags. An hour during your cross-coastal breakup with your university boyfriend—seemingly never-ending. We went through the motions of the weekend, searching for activities to pass the time. I suggested a movie and he suggested lunch. We ended up silently eating cheese bread at Sizzler Innaloo, waiting for the 1.45 p.m. session of *Jason Bourne* to roll around.

I had flown over expecting drama and tears. I had expected to be thrown out of his house, to have to call another Uber. Perhaps the one that had dropped me off would still be nearby.

That would have been absolutely fair and reasonable. In a way this was worse. Silently eating cheese bread surrounded by crazed five-year-olds jacked up on pink lemonade had not been on my break-up bingo card.

It was only on the drive back to his house that my almost-ex-boyfriend's temperament started to change. There were now waves of anger. 'How could I do this to him?' And then the tears came. I held his hand and apologised over and over again.

I knew how this felt. The boyfriend before him had done it to me, and the boyfriend before that. It was the deepest, most crippling pain I had ever felt in my life. It really felt as if those boys had thrust their hands into my rib cage, grabbed my heart and tossed it on the ground. The simple words telling me what they had done had made me feel completely worthless. I was completely worthless. Unlovable.

I hated that I had made him feel this way.

We watched some episodes of *Seinfeld* and fell asleep at seven p.m., at a loss for how to fill any more time. In the morning, we went to a nearby cafe for breakfast and I facilitated an awkward wrap-up of the weekend. I opened the conversation as though I was opening a board meeting: laying out the agenda, re-establishing that I was here not only to confess my sins but to end our relationship. I asked him who he wanted to tell first and how he wanted to tell them. I told him I'd send back anything of his and take anything of mine. We plotted out our plans, paid for breakfast and he drove me to Perth Airport.

When I sat at my gate, I thought about Tom driving back to his house alone. I regretted that I hadn't been more mature, more thoughtful. I wished I was a better person, a person who had spared him that pain. I thought all these things, yet my next act was to go to the airport bar and order a glass of prosecco. I took it back to one of the high tables overlooking the busy terminal, sipped it and scrolled my phone. I was looking for a number: The One. I messaged to tell him the news.

Maybe it was just karma catching up to me, that Christmas day in Paris. Single, sad and alone, in the City of Love, crafting the shittiest moments of my twenty-five years into concise paragraphs in the hope of being cast on a TV program to compete with twenty-eight women for the love and affection of one man. I finished the story about how I had hurt Tom and considered how other people might have filled out this section. Were you meant to be this honest?

I concluded they wouldn't get a true picture of me otherwise and scrolled down.

'What scares you, and why?'

Being alone.

'Please upload a recent photo of yourself. Please do not add filters.'

I scrolled through my camera roll and picked out a cute selfie. I opened Facetune, slimmed my jaw a bit and scrubbed my finger over my teeth and the whites of my eyes to make them look brighter.

I was on the last page. It instructed me to check over my answers before submitting the application. I clicked back through the categories. The Show, Life, Relationships, Future Partner, About You. I wondered if the answers I had given would be enough. Would they like me? Would they see me in the same way that I saw myself? Who were they looking for?

I hit submit.

CHAPTER 2

True Believer

When I was growing up, I would constantly reinvent myself. The first time I did it I was in Year 1. I had decided I didn't like the way my name was spelt anymore: I wanted to be Alicia, not Alisha. Mum still has a full year's worth of schoolwork from that time, which is all consistently labelled with my new, preferred spelling. On a picture of a stick-figure girl standing underneath a rainbow? Alicia. On a handwriting exercise where my pencil traced over dotted cursive lines? Alicia.

I'd done it when I'd changed schools in Year 5. Mum had chosen to repeat me because I'd been struggling to make friends. I was an only child and my lack of siblings meant I hadn't really been socialised. Brothers and sisters let each other know when they're being annoying or too much, but I'd never had that which meant I was very much both of those things. I'd never fit in at my first school. I felt like I was always desperately trying to get the other kids to like me. Mum hoped that trying a new school and holding me back a year would help.

When I rocked up to my new school, I told everyone I was an extremely talented athlete and that I always won age champion at my old school. I said this despite having exercise-induced asthma and barely having run more than one hundred metres in my entire life. I got lucky: I did win age champion, but only by virtue of the fact there were no other thirteen-year-olds at the school. I was the only one in my age group.

In high school, I oscillated between being a troublemaker and trying my best to succeed. I was suspended in Year 8 for drinking vodka at the junior dance and my friends and I once took the liberty of sleeping in our school rowing sheds after a big New Year's Eve but as I neared the final school exams, I decided to apply myself. Throughout Year 11 and Year 12, I put my head down and focused on trying to give myself the best future possible.

I was glad I did because it wasn't until university that I really started to find myself. Where who I was started to line up with who I wanted to be. University was such a shift from high school, where apathy reigned and it was uncool to be passionate. In high school, it was lame to do something you cared about at lunchtime. At university, it was lame if you didn't.

This was nowhere more apparent to me than during Orientation Week at Sydney University. It seemed as though everyone cared, everyone was involved, and everyone was unique. As I walked up towards the imposing quadrangle, I saw a group of students on the lawn bashing each other with foam swords. They were from the Medieval Society. Behind them, performing on a temporary stage, was BarberSoc, an a cappella singing group. The rest of the clubs and societies were set up along Eastern Avenue, the main drag through campus. I joined every second one I walked past. In a matter of hours, I was a member of the university radio station SURG FM, the Sydney University Dramatic Society, the Skiing and Boarding Society (despite having only seen snow twice in my life) and even some of the more niche offerings like the Lawn Bowls Society.

But the stalls that attracted me most were the string of political clubs set up in a row. They were decorated with big, colourful corflutes displaying the name of their party and large cut-outs of their most prominent member politicians.

I stopped at a life-sized Pauline Hanson. It wasn't a One Nation stall; there was no One Nation club on campus. I looked up at the big plastic sign velcroed to the tent. 'Socialist

Alternative', it read. I looked back at the cut-out—there was a big red X drawn across Hanson's face. Her eyes had been scrubbed out with the same Sharpie.

A boy with a sparse dark beard and a buzzcut thrust a leaflet into my hand. He looked a lot older than me—I would've guessed twenty-five—and was talking so fast that all I could catch were the words 'Marxism' and 'Red Flag'. It was a bit overwhelming, so I quickly thanked him and moved down the line. While I wasn't sure whether Socialist Alternative was for me, I did have an inescapable feeling that now I was at university the proper adult thing to do would be to interrogate my values and beliefs and join a political party.

I'd felt affected by politics and political decisions all my life, so it just made sense to try to understand that world. After Mum became pregnant and Dad announced he had a wife, Mum had raised me all by herself. We were a team, best friends. When Mum got breakfast at our local cafe, I chewed on her leftover crusts. When I wanted to see The Wiggles in concert, Mum made sure we had front-row seats. When Mum started a Bachelor of Social Work at Macquarie University, I started at Banksia Cottage, the on-campus childcare centre.

But life as a single mum while studying wasn't easy and for a considerable portion of my childhood we relied on Centrelink and the Salvos as she tried to propel us into safety and stability.

Dotted among Wiggles concerts, tiny tot ballet classes and boundless love were darker periods. There were screaming matches on the phone with my dad, searching for some support after our electricity had been cut off (again). Months spent in a women's refuge in Sydney's heroin-ravaged centre while trying to expedite our housing application. And plenty of 'vegemite sandwich weeks', which was Mum's euphemism for when we'd run out of money for the week. It meant we'd have to wait until either Dad's child support or a Centrelink payment came in.

We eventually did get settled in a community housing unit in the beautiful, leafy suburb of Lane Cove just after my third birthday. But the feeling that life was a little easier for others never really dissipated. By primary school, I had realised that not every family got help from the government and not every family had trouble paying their phone bill. I was amazed at the sheer size of some of my classmates' houses. They had backyards, and those backyards had pools in them. They had Nickelodeon on the TV and owned shirts emblazoned with the Roxy logo. They didn't shop at Vinnies. I oscillated between extreme envy and pride that my mum had created such a wonderful life for us without a lot of money. But the differences remained.

As I approached the end of primary school, kids started talking about where they were going to high school. Many were bound for the elite private schools that dotted the North Shore of Sydney Harbour: Loreto Kirribilli, Wenona, Monte Sant' Angelo. I was familiar with the schools thanks to my afternoon dance classes, where older girls would walk in wearing large backpacks and stiff blazers, leaving them spread around the room when they got changed. All I wanted from high school was to wear a blazer. A blazer meant status. It meant success.

But while my criterion was strictly uniform-based, Mum was pushing to get me into the best school possible that didn't require a house deposit's worth of fees every year. In Sydney, that meant selective public schools, which consistently ranked above private schools for Year 12 outcomes. You had to sit a competitive placement test in Year 6 to get in. Mum put me into tutoring, figuring that the financial sacrifice now was worthwhile to set up my future. I applied myself, acutely aware of how thin she was stretching herself.

Six weeks after I sat the test, kids at school began to receive their results. Once I knew I'd learn my fate in just a handful of days, Mum and I began a new nightly routine. Mum was a beauty therapist, and I'd sit in the back room after school waiting for her to finish her shift. When she was done, she'd drive us home, idle our Mazda 121 at the top of the driveway and I'd jump out and run to the rows of letterboxes, checking ours for the letter.

It came on a Thursday. I stood in the headlight beam from our little car and ripped the envelope open. It was an offer: Sydney Girls High School, in Surry Hills. Receiving that letter, with that offer, felt like I had changed the course of history. There was nothing particularly wrong with the government high schools in my area, but I knew what this meant to Mum. I felt like I had helped her in a really practical way. All she wanted was the best for me. She didn't want me to miss out on any opportunity that would be afforded to someone with a larger home, or bigger bank balance. I was elated, and it got even better: the Sydney Girls High School uniform had a blazer.

Before we graduated, my primary school held an assembly where all the Year 6 students stood on stage in their new high-school uniforms. We clustered according to which school we were attending. A group of kids in blue polo shirts were heading to the local high school. A couple of boys in stiff, straw boaters were going to a private school called Shore. Two girls in long, light-blue dresses were going to Monte Sant' Angelo. The whole event was a parade of what your family could afford and what your future looked like. I stood by myself. I was the only one at my primary school going to Sydney Girls High School.

Mum and I had been to the orientation night the week before. There'd been a stand set up for incoming Year 7 students looking to buy their school uniforms. I was insistent about buying the blazer. I pleaded with Mum. I needed it for the assembly. She tried to explain that we didn't have enough money for every component of the uniform and that it would really look best if I got the tunic with the white shirt to go underneath. She explained that we still needed to buy new school shoes: the new uniform had brown shoes not black. I negotiated: no white shirt, no new shoes, a blazer. That was that. Mum relented. I stood on stage at the school assembly in my black school shoes and an ironed brown tunic with no shirt underneath. The top of my neck was naked where the white collar should have been. Atop my oddly assembled uniform was a brown, crisp blazer. I was so proud.

My pride came from feeling like I'd gamed the system. Despite our financial position or our socio-economic status, I felt like a success. I felt equal to, if not better than, the rows of kids in front of me headed off to private schools across the city. It didn't matter to me that we couldn't afford the shirt.

But what had happened for me wasn't a result of gaming the system at all. It *was* the system. The reason Mum and I were able to survive those early, difficult years was thanks to the social safety net. The reason we had a roof over our heads at all was thanks to the funding of community services. And the reason I was afforded an enviable education was thanks to the establishment of the selective schools system: a ladder of opportunity, open to everyone, regardless of wealth or class. I came to understand that these structures and systems were no accident. They were a series of decisions made by people in power. People in political parties.

I looked back down the line of stalls. The Young Liberals, the Young Greens and Young Labor. My eyes flicked from a vintage corflute of John Howard to the young guy manning the stall. He was wearing a Tony Abbott campaign shirt over a long-sleeved business shirt. I wasn't joining the Young Liberals.

I quickly googled the Greens. I liked a lot of what they stood for but they only had one seat in Parliament. If I was going to join a political party, I wanted it to be one that could do big things, that could change lives. I didn't see how you could do that from the sidelines.

I hovered by the Young Labor stall and a guy introduced himself as Dylan. He told me it was five dollars to sign up and he'd give me a free jumper if I joined. The jumper sealed the deal. I filled out the form and a membership card arrived in the mail a month later.

On campus, politics happened in two places: the Students' Representative Council and the Student Union. The SRC was more focused on activism, while the Student Union ran the clubs and societies program, as well as most of the campus bars.

Both bodies were famed for churning out some of the country's most high-profile politicians—names like Edmund Barton, Anthony Albanese and Malcolm Turnbull. Student politicians took this as evidence of the relevance of what we were doing, and a promise that our names might be famed one day too.

My first dabble in an actual student election was to help my friend Harry, a boy I'd met through legal studies in high school. He'd joined the Labor Party too and now he wanted my help to get elected to the SRC. Harry asked me to meet him at one of the bars on campus called Hermann's. He wanted me to run on his ticket and help him speak to students on Eastern Avenue to convince them to vote. I wasn't really sure what a ticket was, but I liked the idea of being part of something. Harry handed me a purple T-shirt, my first campaign apparel. I held it up. Printed in the centre was a logo of a lion, with marijuana leaves arranged delicately around the mane. 'Legalise It!' the shirt read. His campaign was to legalise weed on campus. I wasn't sure if Harry had even smoked weed before but that was 'beside the point'. 'It will be electorally popular,' he assured me. Harry was right: he was elected to the SRC and that purple T-shirt opened the door to a whole new world for me too.

In many ways, student politics was performance art played out on campus—a miniature version of politics in the real world. Anything that Canberra had, Sydney University did too. Preference deals, privilege, political scandals—we had it all. There was the time a bunch of recently elected Board Directors were booted from the Student Union when it was discovered they had photoshopped receipts in order to appear under the mandated funding cap for the student election, which was 700 dollars. There was another instance when Board Directors were officially censured for the corrupt use of Cabcharges, constituting a few misrepresented trips to go drinking on Oxford Street. And my favourite of them all, the Young Lib who established a new club called the Wine Society, with the sole intention of harvesting members' contact details and convincing them to vote for him in the next Student Union election.

There was plenty of good work too. When the Abbott Government tried to introduce legislation that would deregulate university fees, we all banded together to oppose it. We protested, visited politicians and marched down George Street holding placards. I marched behind the guy with the beard and buzzcut from the Socialist Alternative, whom I'd since developed a bit of a crush on.

All of it—good and bad—was catalogued in the student newspaper, *Honi Soit*. Student politics was covered in a weekly column, my favourite over the years, called 'Gronkwatch'. It wasn't long until I started making my own appearances. Since getting Harry elected to the SRC, I'd become quite the fixture in student politics myself. Just a year and a half after he handed me that purple campaign shirt, I had one of my own. This one was orange, emblazoned with a tiger's scratch and the text *Unleash Alisha*. I was elected president of the Student Union and became deeply involved in Young Labor.

I'd never experienced the sense of belonging I got from Young Labor before. It was like an ultra-nerdy version of those American frat houses and sororities. First-year students were introduced to a mountain of tradition and folklore at student political conferences, where we'd spend our days arguing over massive geopolitical issues and then drink deep into the night.

When everyone was sufficiently boozed, someone would put on 'Khe Sanh' by Cold Chisel and the crowd would erupt after the first iconic chords. They knew every single word. By the chorus, the group would be jumping wildly and pints of beer would be tossed into the air, amber liquid raining down on the crowd. I will never forget the first time I saw it happen; I was captivated by the camaraderie. I wanted to be part of it. I made a note to go home and learn all the lyrics.

The icing on the cake of all this partying was that you still felt like you were working semi-productively towards a career down the track, because in the Labor Party, when you worked hard, you were rewarded. All you had to do was remain loyal. I'd come to learn that loyalty was one of the most important parts of politics, particularly in the faction of the Labor Party I'd joined—Centre Unity. Centre Unity was the right-leaning faction of the Labor Party. It was called Student Unity on campus and Young Centre Unity in Young Labor, but whatever the label, the expectation was the same.

It was an overwhelming culture for someone like me, with my tendency to morph myself into whatever form I thought the collective would be most impressed by. At times, it turned me into a version of myself that I didn't like very much. I would defend things that were indefensible. I would say things that I didn't truly understand, and I would treat people badly in the name of competition or a debate or an election. But my unwavering allegiance to the Party had provided me with the community that I'd never had. And that community, that network, provided opportunities.

My first job in politics was in the NSW Parliament. I worked for Sophie Cotsis, a member of the Upper House. Sophie was kind and supportive and I worked for her every Friday, squeezing my uni tutorials and lectures into the other four days of the week. I'll never forget when she first asked me for my opinion on something that had been swirling around in the media. It wasn't sexy—something like amalgamating local councils—but she asked in such a genuine way and I must have looked taken aback.

'You're my adviser,' she said. 'I care about what you think.'

I appreciated her so much. Because she trusted me, I began to trust myself too. I stayed with her until I graduated. Then I graduated jobs too: to the federal parliament and Bill Shorten's office.

I felt like I'd won the jackpot. A year earlier, I'd been in a Sydney pub frequented by Young Labor when Bill had made an impromptu speech after we'd spotted him, serendipitously walking past, and compelled him over with loud cheers. He'd stood on a chair and addressed the noisy crowd. He'd told us about the Australia he wanted us all to live in. A place where marriage equality was the law. A place where Aboriginal and Torres Strait Islander Australians are part of the national birth certificate: the Constitution. A place where you were defined by your Medicare card, not your credit card. Where, 'no matter who you are, who your parents are, you can have a fair go and get ahead based on how hard you work and how much you care about your fellow Australians'. It was everything I'd joined the Party for. He was a rock star and now I was working for him.

I quickly realised that the reality of working in Canberra was not all impassioned speeches. There was good work but there was also ego, gossip and immense stress. In my role as a media advancer, I was travelling around Australia preparing Bill's events. At times, I'd be flying every single day with no semblance of a routine and without seeing my housemates in Canberra for weeks. We'd travel with big, bulging suitcases and a lectern for press conferences that we had to check in at the oversized baggage counter.

While the bulk of our work was coordinating events, engaging with stakeholders and writing briefs for the office, advancers were best known for trying to keep their bosses away from poor optics—down to the detail of street signs—that could make for embarrassing photos in the paper the next day. The classic example of bad advancing work was Tony Abbott pausing outside The Reject Shop while on the campaign trail. A press-gallery journalist snapped a picture, and it was plastered on the front page of *The Daily Telegraph* the next day, artfully cropped to read 'The Reject'.

Politics is a production and we were the producers. For a good chunk of voters, the six p.m. news is their major touchpoint with politics. It offers the opportunity to broadcast a snappy set of images and soundbites that tell the audience what to think and how to feel. For that reason, it wasn't uncommon to receive a directive asking for the next event to scream 'jobs, jobs, jobs'. Want to let everyone know your candidate is the best person to handle the economy? Pop them in a hard hat in front of a bulldozer. Want the people to know your candidate is caring and thoughtful? Tour a local hospital and, better yet, arrange to speak to a patient.

Back then, I felt advancers didn't command much respect. I noticed that offices predominantly hired young women in the role and I was told this was because young women could more easily flirt, manipulate and negotiate our way out of sticky situations. We could make things happen when they seemed impossible. Advancers didn't seem appreciated in the same way as media or policy advisers were, and promotions or career pathways weren't really on offer. The longer I worked in politics the less I felt the lack of respect was an 'advancer' thing and the more I felt it was a 'woman' thing.

All too often, women in political offices bonded over the shitty things men in politics had done to us. One woman would share a story about how the general secretary of a particular branch of the Labor Party would comment on her outfit each morning as she entered the office. Another would recall a male MP commenting on photos she'd uploaded to her private Facebook account, warning they shouldn't be too sexy as people might get the wrong idea. We would sit over count-less glasses of wine, lamenting the fact that the Opposition Leader's adviser on women's issues was getting paid the same as the receptionist while his other policy advisers were on 40,000 dollars more per annum. We'd analyse our office structure, pointing out that there were only two senior women in a staff of twenty-four. And we'd apologise for being silly as we cried in the toilets after someone moved our things from our desk in the media office to reception, to make way for a 'more senior' man who had just been seconded to work on the election campaign.

That last one was me. It happened about a year into my time with Bill. The man was fine—in fact he was lovely—but it felt emblematic of the challenges of working in a political office. Much of the time the work was rewarding, but there was a constant undercurrent of being undervalued, unappreciated and deemed unimportant.

I'd been working for Bill for just under two years when I submitted my application for *The Bachelor* and it was the first time that I'd fantasised about a different path. I had been so focused on politics: opportunities had come up and I'd taken them. And while I'd appreciated it all, I'd never really stopped to consider whether it was making me happy. I enjoyed the cachet attached to my job: since I'd started getting paid for my activism, friends had become less snarky, more impressed. When I told strangers I worked in Parliament House I could feel that I'd gone up in their estimation. But it wasn't due to anything inherent about me—not because I'd made them laugh, or we'd had a particularly engaging conversation. Just because of my job title. I'd started to wonder if staffing was all that I wanted to do, all I wanted to be.

I'd made some offhand mentions of my *Bachelor* application to a couple of friends, including Lex, but otherwise hadn't given it much thought since coming back to work after the Christmas break. That was until the call came. Lex and I had heard a rumour that Penny Wong, then Leader of the Opposition in the Senate, worked out regularly at the Parliament House gym, so we decided we'd try some classes in the New Year. We were walking back to our office after a surprisingly hard class when my phone rang. As it became apparent who was calling, I flapped my hand wildly against Lex's arm and mouthed 'Oh my god!' while trying to concentrate on the caller.

It was Zoe from Warner Brothers. She was inviting me up to Sydney for a group audition for the next season of *The Bachelor*. It would be in a couple of weeks. She said she would forward the information to the email address they had on file. I got off the phone and repeated the conversation to Lex. We jumped up and down, laughing to ourselves hysterically. I was conscious of the juxtaposition: two twenty-something women dressed in activewear celebrating a call from a reality TV dating show while standing in a hall studded with portraits of Australia's prime ministers. An oil painting of Paul Keating watched on as we made a nuisance of ourselves. I wasn't sure he'd be a fan of the show.

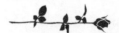

There was no question of whether or not I would go to the audition. It was a story and I was always in search of a good story. Plus, it wasn't like I was going to get it. I'd go to Sydney, have a laugh and then come back on the Murrays bus with a cracking anecdote for future dinner parties. The only problem was the audition was on a workday. We stood in the echoey hall and strategised. I'd throw a sickie, we decided. I never threw sickies, so we rationalised I was practically entitled to one. I would head up after work on Friday and spend the weekend planning my audition approach with my two best friends, Hannah and James. If it was going to be a good story, we agreed, I had to fully commit.

The day before the audition, Hannah, James and I ran through everything I needed to think about, category by category. What I wanted to say, how I should say it. We deliberated over what I should wear. Zoe's follow-up email had said the dress code was what you would wear on a first date. Hannah had lovingly pulled various skirts and dresses from her drawers, ready to style me. But I, wanting to stand out, had already settled on what I should wear. I was planning to wear—I shit you not—a wetsuit. I figured I'd definitely stand out, and when they asked for my justification, I'd lean into the full *Bachelor* date fantasy, telling the casting producer that I imagined our first date would be a surfing lesson, or snorkelling. They'd think I was funny and confident, a manic pixie dream girl for 2018. Hannah and James were not convinced and told me to tone it down.

My second pitch was a cowgirl outfit. It would be more pulled back, I assured them. A little denim skirt, cowboy boots, maybe a hat. It would speak to my country roots, by which I meant yearly visits to Goulburn, where Mum had grown up. There was a rodeo in Goulburn, after all. My first date with the Bachelor could be barrel-racing, or a night under the stars listening to country music. I was basically producing the show for them.

Hannah and James continued to insist that any themed costume was a truly terrible idea, and against my own creative instincts I ended up standing in the room with twenty other women wearing a black T-shirt and a black leather skirt I'd found at Sportsgirl after endless laps of Broadway Shopping Centre.

Our group of twenty, scheduled for five p.m., was the last group of the day. The casting producers had been seeing groups every half hour since nine a.m. That was over 350 people and this was just one day of casting. My adrenaline was pumping as I surveyed the group. Everyone was beautiful. There were nurses and early childhood educators, real estate agents and students. Particularly intimidating was the incredibly toned six-foot-two yoga instructor from Bondi with deep olive-hued skin. She was also nice; she'd complimented my new skirt as we'd waited to be called in. Thank god I wasn't wearing a fucking wetsuit.

In the main casting room stood Meg, the casting director from Warner Brothers. She encouraged us to be ourselves and have fun, gesturing us into a semicircle as she spoke. Once we were assembled, Meg started pointing to girls with her hands pressed together, rapid-firing questions. Her gesture landed on me.

'Introduce yourself,' she said.

'I'm Alisha, I work for Bill Shorten and my ex-boyfriend was a dick,' I responded.

Meg laughed. 'Concise.'

I felt a warm glow creep up my chest and into my cheeks.

Next, we played a game where the casting assistants posed a hypothetical and we stood on the side of the room that represented how we felt about it. 'It's the morning of your best friend's wedding and you walk in on her future husband banging one of her bridesmaids. Do you tell her?' Left—yes, right—no.

The girls separated and I ended up floating about eighty per cent to the left. Meg asked us to justify our position. Again, she picked me. I said I would tell the bride, but I would also support her in whatever decision she made. A few girls nodded supportively, and one slyly scooted a little closer to the left.

To round off the audition, we were split into groups and tasked with choreographing a dance to Ed Sheeran's 'Shape of You'. I found the psychology of these tasks fascinating. As silly as they sound, they provided incredible insight into how everyone operated, the dancing in particular. It was a difficult exercise to do while maintaining a particular persona or pushing particular aspects of your personality. As much as one may have tried to be sweet and agreeable at the start, once paired with three other girls not particularly enthusiastic about the task, one simply can't resist project-managing the whole thing. I was the one project-managing.

Finally, after performing our very amateur dance routines, Meg called on girls to volunteer whom they *wouldn't* want the Bachelor to meet, now that we'd gotten to know each other a little. She picked me first: I chose the yoga instructor. She was simply an all-rounder. There was no way that you'd get any time with the Bachelor after he'd met her. I mean, I was half-thinking *I* wanted to date her. Meg moved on, picking a girl from the other side of the room, who chose me. Meg asked her to justify her choice: it was because of 'my personality'. I didn't know whether to be flattered or not.

With that, the audition was over and we made small talk while Meg conferred with her assistants. She announced to the room that from this group a selection would proceed to an on-camera interview with a panel of producers from the production company, Warner Brothers and the network, Channel Ten. Those selected would have to hang around for a couple of hours while they spoke to everyone chosen from their groups throughout the day.

The room hushed as Meg made her announcement. First, she said the yoga instructor's name and then she said mine. I couldn't believe it. I was chosen. I floated out of the room, intoxicated by Meg's approval. Later, facing the panel of producers, I was called 'refreshing' and I left with an A4 envelope filled with psychometric tests and a compulsory (and very comprehensive) medical to complete over the following weeks.

The feeling of approval was addictive and I loved every part of the audition process. I loved talking to Alex, the show psychologist, unpacking who I was as a person in the hopes of passing her pre-show screening. I loved filling out the pages and pages of paperwork that asked everything from whether I could ice skate to whether I was afraid of heights. I even loved the sense of achievement I felt when my STD check came back clean.

Six weeks after the group audition, I opened my inbox to an email from the Warner Brothers talent and travel manager. 'A BIG, HUGE congrats on making it onto the next series of *The Bachelor*!' it read. I closed my laptop abruptly. I simply could not believe it. My quest for a good story had really snowballed. The idea of going on reality TV had been a fun and easy one when there was no tangible prospect of it actually happening. But now there was an email in my inbox, sitting amid others planning visits to state Labor conferences or marginal electorates. The email from Warner Brothers presented an alternative reality.

I knew I wanted to do it almost immediately. There was just something within me. I loved reality TV. I had grown up on it. I had watched Sara-Marie shake her butt while wearing bunny ears on *Big Brother*. Mum and I had cried big, blubbering tears when Guy Sebastian sang 'Climb Every Mountain' on *Australian Idol* in 2003 and I could still remember the goosebumps I got when Anthony Callea sang 'The Prayer' in 2004. I'd sit on the edge of my seat waiting for Mark Holden to give one of his famous touchdowns, and stay up way past my bedtime to watch the *Up-Late Game Show* with Hotdogs.

There was something special about reality TV, the way it took regular people and turned them into stars. The way Australia embraced all sorts of different characters. I wanted to be a part of it. At the heart of it, I thought, *who gets this? Who truly gets this opportunity to have a crazy adventure? To put themselves out there? To share who they are with the world?*

It spoke to a part of myself that I hadn't really had an opportunity to flex in politics. As a political staffer, you're expected to be neither seen, nor heard. Your opinions are the opinions of the party—that discipline is established at the very beginning, back in student politics. Compared to politics, reality TV seemed like the Wild West, and that was exciting. You could say what you wanted and the stakes were low. You were celebrated for being different or outrageous. It looked like fun.

But I also immediately knew that I might not be able to belong to both worlds.

It wasn't going to be as easy as whipping off my blazer and donning a bikini. I couldn't traipse onto national TV in a ballgown for a couple of weeks and expect no consequences. There was a particular way of doing things in the Labor Party, a way of progressing. You started by volunteering, then perhaps you'd be offered a role in an electorate office, then maybe a ministerial office. If you were interested in being preselected, you'd move into an area where your faction controlled the numbers. Perhaps someplace where the sitting member was getting a bit old. A handful did this while they were still in Young Labor. The most intensely committed structured every part of their lives around progression through the Party. Jokes were common about 'corflute wives' or 'corflute babies', implying that particular life events were timed for what would look good on a piece of election material. Whatever the case, be it moving or marriage, you most certainly did *not* go on a reality TV show.

I'd also need to ask for significant time off, which wasn't something any boss took lightly. But I figured staffers shuffled offices and roles in the Labor Party all the time. People went on junkets under the guise of 'researching democracy' or took extended leave because they wanted the gap year they'd never had. I'd seen other people offered these opportunities, so I decided there was some hope.

After floating the news with some supportive people and letting it settle, I raised the idea with Bill Shorten's chief of staff. I requested some time in his diary and we met with takeaway coffees in hand near a water feature in a garden adjacent to our office. The news fell out of my mouth almost comically.

'I applied to go on *The Bachelor* and I've gotten on,' I said.

I could see in his eyes that it was the last thing he'd been expecting to hear. 'And you want to do it?' he responded.

'I think I do,' I said.

Before he could continue, I pitched to him the idea that I could go on leave without pay. I spoke fast, filling the silence, explaining that I'd spoken to some of the advance team and they thought they could handle the load. We weren't anywhere close to the election and the first part of the parliamentary year was quiet. I told him I didn't think I'd be gone for long, a couple of weeks max.

He was truly perplexed. This was a guy who sat in briefings with shadow ministers, fielding questions about campaign strategy and complex issues, not proposals for his staff to go on *The Bachelor*. He looked at me, searching for a response. I'd stumped a person who had an answer for everything. When he did gather his thoughts, he was completely reasonable and diplomatic. He told me he'd need to talk to a couple of people in the office but it wasn't a no.

Buoyed by this, I let myself get a little too excited. I even began plotting how Bill Shorten—*the* Bill Shorten—could be included in those introductory scenes a handful of the contestants on *The Bachelor* get. When I started fielding phone calls from *Bachelor* producers, we spitballed the idea of flying a crew to Canberra. We could set up outside Parliament House, shooting back towards the building from the forecourt. I looked up the filming protocols for Parliament House and even sent a very vague email to someone in the Department of Parliamentary Services. I kept Bill's chief of staff in the loop, but he remained noncommittal. I thought it was a good sign. Maybe it wouldn't have to be one or the other. Maybe I could have it all. It would be easy: I could go off, shoot *The Bachelor* and come back home to my job, ready to help elect the next prime minister of Australia.

From my perspective, I was a valued member of the office, trotting off to do something crazy and exciting. Why wouldn't they support me? We were a family, a Labor family.

From their perspective, I was a liability.

Bill's chief of staff didn't give me an answer on whether I could keep my job and do the show until six days before I was meant to fly out to film.

The last few weeks in Parliament House had been wild. A story had broken in *The Daily Telegraph* about Deputy Prime Minister Barnaby Joyce's former staffer Vikki Campion. She'd been snapped by a press-gallery photographer walking through Canberra in a striped T-shirt and black sports shorts—with a baby bump. She was pregnant with Joyce's child. This set off a chain of events throughout Parliament House culminating in a 'bonk ban' announced by Prime Minister Malcolm Turnbull.

The mood was tense and it was spilling over everywhere, even into Budget Estimates, where Liberal Employment Minister Senator Michaelia Cash, unhappy while being grilled about an entirely different matter, publicly threatened to 'name every young woman in Mr Shorten's office over which rumours in this place abound'.

When I met again with Bill's chief of staff, it became clear that things had changed during the intervening four weeks. The political landscape was more turbulent and the people he had consulted had strong opinions. He was no longer noncommittal. He rattled off a list of concerns around 'optics', 'perception' and what it would mean for the Party. He told me the idea was no longer feasible. We had reached an impasse.

An unspoken word lingered over the conversation: resignation.

Suddenly, I had a decision to make: reality TV or politics. I couldn't do both. I had given so much time and energy to the Labor Party and Young Labor. I had spent so many years establishing myself as trustworthy and loyal, and I'd finally started doing the work we all hoped to do. It felt like good, important work. Work that would have helped people like me and Mum, back when we really needed it. Was I really going to throw that all away for an opportunity to appear on a TV show?

But I had a more complex relationship with the Labor Party than when I'd first joined. Parliament House wasn't the beacon of probity and progress I'd once thought. At times, working in politics could make you feel like a shell of yourself. Parties demanded so much from individuals but didn't allow much room for people to be the individuals they were. Reality TV felt like an opportunity to be my full self, to share my full personality, without worrying about whether I was on message.

I also worried about what people would think of me. I knew the consensus opinion of people who went on reality TV: fame-hungry, self-centred, the worst kind of egotists, who sought out shows like *The Bachelor* specifically to gain a following on social media, only to monetise it flogging skinny tea to impressionable sixteen-year-olds.

It was what I thought about reality TV contestants too. I'd completely absorbed society's narrative about who these people were. That the women had big bolt-on boobs, that the men had blindingly white teeth and that none of them had a whole lot going on upstairs. Those characteristics meant they mustn't be good people, that we were all somehow better than them. Just months before I'd submitted my *Bachelor* application, a reporter for the *Daily Mail* had been fired because they'd accidentally published an article describing reality TV stars as 'vapid cunts'. I'd laughed when I'd seen it on Twitter, copied the link and sent it to my group chat. 'Where's the lie?' had been my accompanying message.

And it wasn't just the superficial stuff. I feared that by going on *The Bachelor* I might start to disassemble, brick by brick, the foundation of who I was. The values I'd collected throughout my life and the beliefs I'd sifted through during orientation week, trying to figure out where I sat on the political spectrum. I felt like my identity was held together by a bunch of '-ists'—activist, unionist, feminist—and I worried that *The Bachelor* might be the antithesis of everything that I thought—and wanted—myself to be.

I sat on my bed the night after the conversation with Bill's chief of staff and started to google key phrases: 'Feminism and *The Bachelor*', 'Capitalism and *The Bachelor*', 'Clementine Ford and *The Bachelor*'. I opened a bunch of tabs and began to read through them. I didn't trust my own judgement—I needed to outsource the decision to people I perceived to be smarter, more respected. I needed them to tell me it was okay to do the show. I read article after article, soon realising that I was gravitating towards those that supported my true desire. Ones titled '9 Reasons Strong, Intelligent, Feminist Women Watch *The Bachelor*' or 'The Surprisingly Feminist Roots of *The Bachelorette*'. It was clear I wanted to do the show.

By the end of the week, I'd handed in my formal resignation. Later that day, I composed a text to Bill saying what a privilege it had been to work in his office for the past two years and that I looked forward to seeing him become the next prime minister of Australia.

He never replied.

CHAPTER 3

The Mansion

I approached the days before flying to Sydney to shoot the show as though I was cramming for the biggest exam of my life. Lex invited me over to her apartment in Kingston to prep. I scanned the Wikipedia pages of past seasons looking for patterns, while she poured us glasses of wine. I knew the archetypes and I wondered where I'd fit. You wanted to be a wifey, the one that gets the soft, sparkly music when the season goes to air. They get the single dates, the roses at the start of the rose ceremony and they're the ones still standing at the end.

The show was easy to analyse because it was so formulaic, down to the same types of characters being eliminated in the same episode each season.

'The villains are usually eliminated halfway through,' I told Lex matter-of-factly, as Matty J's season of *The Bachelor* played in the background.

'Remember Keira Maguire?' I said. 'She got booted on episode eight.'

Keira was one of the original and iconic villains of the franchise. She'd been destroyed in the media at the time her series aired but I always found her compelling. She had a no-fucks attitude, which I admired, and she was full of personality. I'd always been more attracted to the villains. They seemed to have more depth.

I didn't want to be one though. I wanted to be successful. I wanted to be loved. I wanted to win.

On Sunday, 11 March 2018, my alarm jolted me awake at five-thirty a.m. It was the morning of my flight to Sydney. I had a habit of setting alarms unnecessarily early when I was anxious or unprepared. This morning I was both. I was booked on QF1474 Canberra to Sydney, departing at 12.05 p.m. I'd laid two suitcases out on my bedroom floor and they were brimming with piles of clothes assembled by category. Shorts, shirts, skirts and dresses. Another suitcase was stacked with a pile of colourful gowns gently folded in half, still on their hangers. The packing list from Warner Brothers had specified that we needed to bring a minimum of five dresses appropriate for a cocktail party so I'd spent the last forty-eight hours negotiating with people on Facebook Marketplace who were selling their old formal dresses, and driving to the far reaches of Canberra to pick them up.

I'd also woken early because I needed to do a last-minute run to Woolies for toiletries. I scanned the packing list I'd printed off at work before I'd resigned for items I needed to buy: toothbrush, toothpaste, deodorant, shampoo and conditioner. I actually had most of these in the bathroom already but they were all half-empty and gross. It didn't feel right to bring them into this new experience, into the *Bachelor* mansion. Everything I brought needed to reflect the best version of myself, down to my toothbrush.

As I reached the self-service check-out, I was stopped by what would soon become a very familiar face, gracing the front of a stack of *Daily Telegraph* newspapers. Hair in ringlets, wiry ginger moustache and a trademark headband made of foam and electrical tape: Nick Cummins, commonly known by his nickname, the Honey Badger. He was usually featured in the sports pages at the back of the paper, but here he was smack bang on the front, holding a rose. There was constant theorising in the media about who the next Bachelor might be, but this looked like a legitimate announcement, photo shoot and all.

I was surprised. It was a new direction for the show, which generally stuck to a very predictable blueprint in casting the lead. Clean-cut men with aspirational careers and chiselled abs. What the production company thought women should want. The Honey Badger wasn't radically different, but he was unexpected and I saw it as refreshing.

I knew the Honey Badger was a rugby union player, but not much more than that, so I hovered beside the stack of papers googling his name. The little I knew about him from the media came back pretty quickly. He was the personification of a Banjo Paterson poem, beloved by Australian men, celebrated for his larrikinism and one-liners. A three-minute YouTube video compiled his 'funniest moments'.

'When the start of the season turns up, the boys will be going off like a bull in a china shop.'

'Last year we were all sizzle and no steak.'

'He was sweating like a bag of cats at a greyhound meet.'

He was definitely unlike previous Bachelors and I was into it. I kept scanning through videos and articles about Nick as

I sorted out my suitcases and jumped into a cab to Canberra airport. There, I started a clip from *Sunday Night*, a current affairs program on the Seven Network. It covered Nick's decision to retire from rugby at the peak of his career, in large part because his father, Mark, had received a terminal prostate cancer diagnosis. The story followed Mark, Nick and two of his brothers, Joe and Luke, on a special trip through the Kimberley.

Nick's voice narrated: 'Family is number one. That's flat out it.'

I felt an immediate tenderness towards him. His story resonated with me. Mum had lost her own dad, my grandpa, years earlier in part due to prostate cancer. Nick was one of eight kids; my Pa was the youngest of thirteen. I closed the tab before the video finished, deciding I wanted to learn everything else about him organically. I watched Canberra whirr past the window of the car and flirted with the idea that this could be the start of something. Maybe we'd actually click.

When I landed in Sydney, I was greeted by a very flustered woman called Izzy. She was surrounded by a handful of girls all armed with two suitcases. Izzy was an assistant producer, charged with wrangling us into a white van to take us to our next location. 'Don't talk to each other,' she said with a strong English accent through gritted teeth. 'You're not meant to know each other!' She looked just like one of the producers from the popular series *UnREAL*, which provided a behind-the-scenes glimpse into a fictitious dating show modelled closely on *The Bachelor*. I always thought that the show embellished the truth but here Izzy was, dressed all in black, a walkie-talkie on her hip, earpiece in her ear. In the van, she passed around a pile of black hoodies and instructed us to put them on with the pair of sunglasses we'd been told to pack in our carry-on. Giggles and murmurs of 'paps' and 'the *Daily Mail*' reverberated through the van as we awkwardly negotiated getting our limbs into the hoodies in the tight space.

Our next location wasn't the famous Bachelor mansion as we'd assumed; it was Quest Apartments, a nondescript high-rise in Chatswood in Sydney's north. We were told we'd be there for three days, holed up in a hotel room with just one other contestant. Three days without our phones, internet or TV.

It was called the sequester. I learnt production sequestered contestants before shooting reality TV shows for a range of reasons. For our season they conducted twenty-eight individual hour-long 'master' interviews during which the producers unpicked each element of our personality: they asked us our biggest regrets, whether we considered ourselves competitive, and why we were still single. We had meetings with the wardrobe department. And we had a big group briefing about how shooting would work, what the contracts we had all signed meant and what would happen if we broke them.

The sequester also served to disconnect us from the real world and our real lives, transitioning us to the *Bachelor* bubble, where there were new rules.

My roommate for the three days was Autumn. She was from Melbourne, and a little bit older than me. I was twenty-five, she was twenty-nine. She was nothing like what I was expecting. I'd been primed to think all the women I'd be competing against would be shallow and narcissistic, but Autumn was warm and curious. We swapped stories about our dating histories, life and work over the hours we were locked in our room until we had a full tapestry of knowledge about one another.

I don't know whether it was her age or disposition, but Autumn was way more chill about meeting the Bachelor than I was. For me, it felt like a make-or-break life event. It had to go well, and I had to impress him. My biggest fear was being eliminated on the first night. I couldn't even fathom the humiliation of returning to Canberra after just a handful of days. Autumn was unbothered. She seemed more focused on whether the Bachelor would be good enough for her.

We traded our plans for what we were going to do on the red carpet. Producers had been ringing us over the past few weeks, workshopping our entrances, which were intended to give a bit of insight into who we were. Autumn's idea was awesome. She was a graphic designer by trade and before she'd flown to Sydney, she'd sketched a vector-style rose and had it made into a temporary tattoo. She was going to apply it to her thigh where the split in her dress was and tell the Bachelor there was a clue about what she did for work somewhere on her body. I was jealous; Autumn's entrance was sexy and smart. I hadn't come up with anything that good. In fact, it felt like I'd just been rebuffing my producer's ideas. I told Autumn about my producer's first suggestion: 'She said I should walk up to him, put a piece of duct tape over both our mouths and then just stare into his eyes for a couple of minutes,' I said. 'What the actual fuck.'

In the producer's mind, it was meant to be a call back to when Merlin from *Big Brother* staged a silent protest at his eviction, in which he'd covered his mouth with black tape and held up a sign reading FREE TH[E] REFUGEES: 'That's a political message and you work in politics,' the producer had said. I thought she was setting me up to be a laughing-stock. I'd done my research; I knew the girls who did novelty entrances never made it to the end.

I'd managed to appease the producer at the time by saying I'd try to get the Bachelor to take his shirt off, 'or something', which I now deeply regretted. I was so nervous about the whole thing that I ended up scripting out an entire interaction in a notebook I'd brought with me, down to cues as to when I should touch his arm, or when I should laugh. I was right to be anxious.

When the time came for us to meet the Bachelor, a producer mustered me to get into the limo that had been motoring up and reversing back down the same stretch of driveway all night. She told me that I'd have ten minutes with the Bachelor when I met him, which was far more than I'd expected. I'd thought it would be as brief as it looked on TV—'Hello, I'm Alisha, nice to meet you, see you inside'—and I was panicked to learn that it would be so much longer.

My introduction was not ten minutes. It was short and it was awkward. The Honey Badger was waiting for me on the red carpet, and I greeted him way too enthusiastically, nothing like the sweet, demure character I'd rehearsed. I decided to open with one of his own one-liners telling him I was 'as nervous as a long-tailed cat in a room full of rocking chairs'. He laughed with me kindly, clearly sensing my nerves. I searched for what to say next, thinking back to my script. The shirt. I encouraged him to take his jacket off. It was weird. I could tell he wasn't that into it, so I didn't push it any further. After a total of two a half minutes, I wrapped it up with a 'see you inside!' and almost sprinted up a pebbled path towards a waiting production assistant. They motioned me towards a waiting camera and boom mic. It was my first voxxie: a short, in-the-moment inter-view, intended to capture how I felt about our interaction. I think I knew from that very first conversation that there wasn't a spark between us but I didn't want it to be true. I was resolute that I could shift reality.

A producer called Dean opened the voxxie enthusiastically. 'What do you think?!'

'He was amazing,' I gushed. 'So warm and so lovely. I think we really clicked.'

I said everything that I wanted to be true. I needed to position myself as a contender, someone who could be standing with Nick at the end. I hoped Dean would believe it.

After a couple more questions, he let me loose into a court-yard decked out with thousands of fairy lights; at least a dozen other women were already there. I spied Autumn across the space and we debriefed our entrances. Hers had gone really well. *Of course, it did*, I thought, *she was so smooth*. We were all left to get to know each other for a couple of hours while the crew wrapped up the rest of the arrivals. It mostly felt like a really good party. Nothing felt real until the longstanding host of the franchise, Osher Günsberg, entered, tapping a champagne flute with his wedding band. The twenty-eight women clustered around an assortment of velvet couches as Osher welcomed our Bachelor. Nick gave a short speech about the type of love he was looking for, before flirting with the group of women closest to him. I could see the particular women he was noticing, taking in their physicality. I immediately felt insecure.

A month earlier I'd stood in front of my friend James in a sports bra and undies and asked him what he thought of my body. James was about as direct as you could get and I'd decided he was my best shot at an honest appraisal. I'd turned to the left, sucking my stomach in slightly as I moved. My hair was in a messy bun and I pressed my tongue to the top of my mouth because years ago I'd read in *Cosmopolitan* it would make my jawline look more sculpted. I hated my profile, mostly for my nose but also because I thought I had a bit of a double chin. I'd read in the same magazine that you could get injections of something called deoxycholic acid to treat 'submental fat'—it promised to rid me of that fat pocket under my chin I hated— but I wasn't very good with pain so I'd flipped over to an article about hand jobs being sexy again.

James had said that I looked great but appeased me by saying he understood why I might want to tone up a bit. We had pushed his three-seat couch and heavy second-hand coffee table into the corner of the room and I stood against the living room wall, handing him my iPhone so he could take a series of 'Before' photos. I didn't really think I would stack up looks-wise to the women who appear on *The Bachelor*, with their tiny figures, gorgeous voluminous hair and button noses. They were effortlessly beautiful and the women gathered around the velvet couches seemed to confirm that.

Beauty didn't feel effortless to me, it felt *full* of effort—continual effort that consumed so much of my time and energy. For as long as I could remember I had been trying to make little tweaks to my appearance, thinking that maybe with slightly longer eyelashes, slightly more sun-kissed skin, or finally dropping those five kilograms, I would unlock some bonus level of confidence and fulfilment. Things would come more easily. I'd be permanently happy.

I knew I wasn't meant to think this way. Every time I opened Instagram, I was told I should embrace the skin I'm in, that I don't exist solely to lose weight and be pretty. I knew that and it made me even more frustrated that the thoughts were there. But I couldn't escape them, so leading into the show I'd put into practice all the toxic tips and tricks I'd accumulated over the years. By the time I was twelve, I'd accompanied my mum to more WeightWatchers meetings than I could count on both hands. She'd also always been trying to lose five kilos. There, I'd heard that veggies were good and carbohydrates were bad, so in preparation for the show I started eating the same meal of salmon and broccoli each and every night. I'd also put 4000 dollars on a credit card to bankroll a new set of hair extensions, lash extensions and a new wardrobe of clothes.

Observing Nick and the girls around him, it felt like I'd achieved nothing; I felt just as average as when I'd started. By now Nick had focused on a girl called Rhiannon, whom I'd met earlier that evening. She was a Pilates instructor and was wearing one of the most show-stopping dresses of the night: long-sleeved black velvet, with a deep V-neck. They laughed together at something I wasn't able to overhear. Then his hand reached for her arm and he asked her for a chat.

That first cocktail party was shot over two nights and our first rose ceremony rounded off the second. We lined up across a small staircase within a small room decorated in the most gauche, maximalist style you can imagine. We were instructed to stand in three rows and find a gap between the two women in front of us so our faces could be seen by five cameras.

On TV it takes fifteen minutes, but in reality the exercise went on for hours. The Bachelor was directed to pause as he picked up each rose. To move his fingers up to the petals, look down at the rose thoughtfully and then back up to the girls. Then a name would be read to him over his earpiece. It was an agreed-upon list, constructed after consultation with the producers. Nick called the name Brittany first, then Dasha, then Kayla, then Rhiannon. I was a little further down the order but breathed a sigh of relief at being safe. The names continued until there were no roses left to give. I stretched to see who was still standing: Susie, Urszula and Autumn. I felt a wave of panic, projecting my own fears of going home first onto my roommate. I couldn't believe she hadn't received a rose. I didn't understand the decision-making. Autumn was smart, funny and gorgeous. Suddenly it all seemed very arbitrary. The girls who had been picked shuffled forwards to say goodbye to the three who didn't receive a rose and, when she was cued by production, Autumn thanked Nick and walked out into the night, her *Bachelor* experience bundled into a handful of hours.

Filming wrapped at five a.m. We practically ripped off the heels that had been torturing us. Eyes nodded closed as audio guys tried to respectfully remove the microphones sticky-taped down our dresses. As dawn broke, we piled into mini-vans to shuttle back to Quest for one last night. I thought about the girls that had left. Popped into black sedans with a producer, to extrapolate on their humiliation. I felt bad for them; the whole thing felt completely dehumanising, but I couldn't deny a simmering feeling of superiority. I'd been chosen. I looked around the van. Someone—be it the Bachelor or the producers—had decided it was worthwhile to keep us around, that there was something interesting about us. A shared sense of relief hung in the air as a greasy bag of hash browns was passed from girl to girl.

We would officially move into the mansion the next day.

The *Bachelor* mansion was nestled in a quiet corner of Sydney's Northern Beaches. Warner Brothers rented it from the owner for three months every year. Its usual styling was a bit Hamptons, a bit Southern with a dash of nautical, but once the TV crew moved in it became somewhat of a Potemkin village. Everything looked great on the outside, all manicured lawns and decadent set dressing, but behind the curtain, life was far less glamorous. The three main bedrooms were packed with rows and rows of bunk beds to sleep the twenty-five girls. I slept in a top bunk above Dasha, a single mum from Sydney's Eastern Suburbs who was already an extremely successful fitness influencer. We were in the main bedroom, home to twelve girls. There was one bathroom between us, and we soon learnt to negotiate the morning rush before a day of filming. Shooting often only took up a small fraction of each day, so the girls spent the bulk of their time sitting around watching movies or sunbathing by the pool. Some had taken to sunbathing topless to avoid tan lines but this was quickly halted by production once they found out the tabloids had been flying drones over our backyard. It didn't take long until we were all deeply bonded, a process that was sped along by a session of trauma-bonding that Brooke Blurton, a soon-to-be season frontrunner and future Bachelorette, had facilitated on our first night. All twenty-five of us had sat around an outdoor setting and shared the most vulnerable chapters of our lives—parents divorcing, abusive relationships, eating disorders. One by one, we opened up to each another, finding solidarity in each other's stories. I remember thinking that it was nothing like viewers of the show would've imagined. It was nothing like *I'd* imagined. In this group of women at least, there was not one vapid cunt among us. Moments like these weaved their way through the six weeks I spent in the *Bachelor* mansion. While we were purportedly there to find love with an ex-rugby union player, the real magic of it all was the relationships we started to build with each other and the production crew that ran the whole operation.

Romy Poulier and Cat Henesey-Smith were to become my closest friends in the mansion.

Romy was an absolute bombshell. She had ice-blue eyes that were usually framed with a bit of smoky black eyeliner, Marilyn Monroe lips, and platinum blonde hair sitting just below her shoulders. I'd expected to hate Romy because of how beautiful she was, but it was impossible not to like her.

When you talked to her, she made you feel like you were saying the most interesting things she'd ever heard. When I told her I lived in Canberra, she wanted to know exactly when I'd moved there and why. When I told her I worked in politics, she wanted an hour-long explainer on the Westminster system and how preferential voting works. Her genuine curiosity made you feel instantly bonded to her, wanting to pour out more of your life to see what she made of it.

Cat—who would come to be known as Cat from Bali when the series aired—was charismatic and confident, but above all else she was funny. She was always telling some outrageous story about high school or her dating escapades, yet she could just as easily slip into an extraordinarily nuanced conversation. One moment you'd be in stitches as she told stories of sneaking out at thirteen, the next you'd be deep in a discussion about how she negotiated cultural differences with her Indonesian ex-boyfriend.

One of our first 'activities' in the mansion was a press shoot for Channel Ten. We'd been briefed the night before that we'd need three outfits—a white top and blue jean combo, a casual, day-date look and a cocktail party look. The girls were frantic, and the subsequent hours blurred into one of those kitsch wardrobe montage scenes that featured in almost every noughties rom-com, where the protagonist tries on everything in their closet and the supporting cast review each look with a thumbs up or thumbs down. Despite everyone bringing two swollen suitcases to the mansion, we all suddenly had nothing to wear. Dresses, tops and accessories flew around the room as we bartered with each other for a cute shirt or denim cut-offs. I had a pair of white Supre skinny jeans that I thought were an absolute serve. I just needed the perfect top to style them with. One of my new friends, Renee, gave me a free pass at her suitcase, and on finding a stretchy green bandeau top, I presented my proposed look to the group of girls clambering in their own cases. 'What do we think of this?' I asked.

'Not unless you want to look like you're the sixth member of Bardot,' Cat responded, referencing the iconic late nineties girl group. The delivery was just perfection—so cold but so accurate—we all burst into fits of laughter. Cat was right. It wasn't a look. There was something about her honesty that just connected me to her. She was the girlfriend everyone wanted to have—the person who can tell you that something looks terrible on you, without making you feel belittled or insecure. Romy was the same. There was no pretence with them, they told you exactly what they thought, and you knew exactly who they were. Romy, Cat and I became a bit of a unit, our friendship deepening over many episodes of *Law & Order: Special Victims Unit* and a shared crush on a producer we called 'Hot

Tom'—a tall, charming guy from Manchester whom we were all convinced was flirting with us and us alone.

Other small groups were established as well, as girls naturally gravitated towards one another. Britt, Sophie and Cass were three of the girls who seemed to be getting most of the attention from the Bachelor. Britt had received the first rose at our first rose ceremony, Sophie had received one-on-one time during our first group date, and at every cocktail party it seemed as though Cass was having hour-long conversations with Nick.

Increasingly, I started to feel like I was fading into the background and, increasingly, I became sensitive to that fact. This came to a head in everyday moments. When the producers set us up for a scene in the living room in preparation for the arrival of a date card, they would only put microphones on a select few girls. The rest they captured with a big boom mike that hovered overhead. When I first realised I wasn't being mic'd up, I ran to one of the bathrooms and started to cry, fearing my irrelevance. I re-emerged when the date card was read and then, registering that my name wasn't included, I headed back to the bathroom at the earliest opportunity.

By the time the fourth cocktail party rolled around, and I'd only been selected for one group date, I decided I needed to reintroduce myself. I didn't feel like Nick actually knew anything about me yet. I wasn't sure if he even knew my name.

So I workshopped an idea with Cat and Romy: I was planning to share the 'layers of my life'. Over my cocktail party dress, I pulled on my 'Unleash Alisha' campaign shirt from my time in student politics. On top of that I put a Canberra Raiders jersey, a nod to both my home and my NRL team. On my feet, I had a pair of treasured oversized Ugg boots, which used to belong to my Pa. I looked like an absolute laugh but I thought it would be a fun way to step Nick through some of the things that had made me who I was, ending by sharing with him how difficult it had been to lose Pa and how much I admired that his family clearly meant so much to him. I hoped by opening up a little I'd manage to connect with him more.

On spying my elaborate costume, a producer sidled up and asked me to run him through my plan. He jumped in at the end.

'Let's lose the grandpa thing,' he said. 'Too heavy. Let's keep it fun, keep it light.'

I hadn't been expecting that response; I'd thought I would be encouraged to share more of myself with Nick. But I didn't want to go against the producer so when I asked Nick for a chat, the Ugg boots went unmentioned. I teased him about my NRL jersey, peeled it off and told him about working in politics. His gaze hovered past me to his own producer for the duration of our conversation, until he slapped his hand on my knee mid-sentence.

'Great getting to know you,' he said abruptly, before moving on to the next girl.

That's when I really started to spiral. In my interviews with the producers, I noticed I was no longer being asked about my connection with Nick. Those questions had been replaced with whether I thought a particular girl's behaviour was disrespectful, or whom I considered the biggest threat. I worried that answering the questions in an indirect way would make me redundant, so I started to give the producers what I thought they wanted. I pushed a little harder, made my commentary a little spicier, my jokes a little darker.

I got a laugh. I kept getting laughs. The producer's laugh was addictive. Even better I was starting to be rewarded. Now when we set up for a scene in the living room, my favourite audio guy, Reuben, waved a mic in the air beckoning me. Being recognised by production was a salve to my insecurity. I thought that being somebody was better than being nobody. Now I was useful, somebody adding to the story and keeping things exciting. My compliance bought me a couple more weeks.

By my sixth week in the mansion, I'd only spoken to the Bachelor for all of twenty minutes and I'd come to terms with the fact that I wasn't considered a contender for his heart. I stood quietly through rose ceremony after rose ceremony, waiting to learn my fate, expecting the worst every time. By that point,

I was just happy to be there. In fact, I had a growing feeling that I'd overstayed my welcome, that I was holding on by a thread. So, I stood with fingers crossed, hoping I'd done enough. Hoping to continue to collect my ninety dollars a day—because, god knows, I didn't have a job waiting for me when I left.

While I grappled with my rejection in silence, Cat struggled more outwardly. When three new contestants arrived on set and frontrunner Brooke received her second single date, she broke down in tears. A second date is presented to the audience as a sign that things are getting serious for the Bachelor, but to the girls who have been there for weeks, seeking a crumb of connection, it feels like a slap in the face. A symbol of your worthlessness. When they saw that Cat was not taking the news well, producers ushered her, Romy and I into a scene together by the pool in the middle of the mansion. Cat vented her frustration, said she felt overlooked. She felt she wasn't going to have an opportunity to share who she really was with the Bachelor and that the whole experience was just another rejection to add to her list. Watching other girls, week after week, be selected for dates, leave the mansion and return with stories about a sunset hot-air balloon ride or sharing a kiss on Sydney Harbour had officially broken her. She floated the idea of giving Nick an ultimatum at the next cocktail party, asking him straight out whether he was interested in getting to know her or she would leave. She'd go back to her support network, pick up the pieces after being rebuffed and carry on.

The ultimatum did not go as Cat had hoped. She didn't even get to deliver it. At the cocktail party that night, when Cat and Nick sat down to have a chat, Nick led the conversation. He said that he'd heard there was growing commotion in the mansion and that Cat's name kept coming up in his conversations. 'I can't deal with that anymore because it's stopping me from possibly finding the girl of my dreams,' he told her. Then he closed with, 'Cat, I think it's time to leave.'

Cat was escorted to a waiting limo and in the rose ceremony that night I didn't receive a rose and Romy left too.

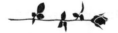

Romy and I were piled into a mini-van to head back to the Quest one last time. Before the heavy door slid shut, a production assistant popped in with sandwich bags labelled with our names. Our passports, our wallets and our phones. Everything that had been taken from us at the start. Production had kindly charged our phones and I was overwhelmed by the number of notifications. When I peeked at my texts there was name after name, all accompanied by messages with lots of capital letters and exclamation marks. I decided to google my name before I read them all. My double-barrelled last name made the results very specific. Ordinarily, the results were an eclectic bunch. There was a link to my Pinterest board: a time capsule from 2012, stuffed with pictures of statement necklaces, tube skirts and inspirational quotes. There were links to a handful of articles from my time in student politics, some more embarrassing than others. If you clicked to page two of the results, you'd find a link to a defunct website called Ice Models. The page featured a series of headshots of me aged fifteen in a red pleather jacket. I'd paid 300 dollars for the headshots under the illusion that I'd been scouted for a modelling agency. The pictures had been taken in a tiny studio above a supermarket in the middle of Sydney's CBD. The whole operation had been a scam: they'd told me they were going to pitch me for jobs and I'd never heard from them again. I used to dread what an employer outside the Labor Party would think if they saw those. Now they were going to see an entirely different picture of me.

One search result sat above all the rest: 'Alisha Aitken-Radburn, *Bachelor* Australia, Season 6, Page 2'. It was a forum for *Bachelor* fans. I clicked through. The first post in the thread was from a user called Bobette. They linked an article published by the *Daily Mail* while the show had been shooting. 'Another contestant has been named: Alisha Aitken-Radburn,' Bobette wrote. '*DM* says she works in politics . . . Politicians are generally not popular in AU—she might have been cast as a villain.'

Villain. It was so conclusive. I felt my face get hot and quickly looked out the window into the dark night to conceal my sudden emotion from Romy. I was self-aware enough to know I hadn't been an angel on the show. There had been conflict at cocktail parties, heated arguments in the house and I had really hitched my wagon to Cat and Romy, who I knew had flown very close to the sun with some of their comments in interviews. But outside of filming everything seemed calm and fun. I was leaving the experience with a list of the girls' phone numbers, Instagram handles and emails to get in touch as soon as I returned to the 'real world'. 'Villain' didn't seem to match up with that, but there was something about reading the word that now seemed inevitable.

I looked back down at my phone; the post went on. 'Does anyone else find it weird that she isn't really smiling in any of her IG pics? Maybe she's self-conscious about her teeth but it makes her look a bit smarmy and disingenuous, IMO.'

Bobette was right. I was self-conscious about my teeth. I thought they were too small and never white enough. I had always thought that smiling without my teeth was more flattering, but now that they said it looked smarmy, I made a mental note to try to start smiling with my teeth.

The rest of the thread was mostly conjecture about whether I had been eliminated yet. Bobette and another user, DirtyStreetPie, posted pictures of group dates they'd found on paparazzi sites, dates I hadn't even been on. It was so comprehensive—I was captivated. DirtyStreetPie thought I'd gone weeks ago, posting a photo of my castmates lined up in a row. She'd numbered their heads to provide a consistent identification system. 'Alisha may be out?' it read underneath.

Bobette replied, 'Kind of feel bad for the girl—she quit her job to go on the show (and the position was advertised last week, so she's probably already been replaced) and for what? A week on a reality TV show where your character can be manipulated into whatever the producers choose to portray? Not a wise career move if you want to continue in the field of politics.'

I felt my stomach drop.

CHAPTER 4

The Aftermath

When I returned home to Canberra, it was to no job, little-to-no savings and no future plan. Canberra felt uncomfortable. About six weeks earlier the gossip had done the rounds of Parliament when the *Daily Mail* had published a detailed line-up of *The Bachelor*'s female contestants, complete with very unflattering pictures snapped by a long lens pointed up at our balconies at Quest. A source had told the *Daily Mail* that an email had been sent around the Leader of the Opposition's office saying that I'd left to 'pursue a project'.

My only reason for living in Canberra was my work with the Labor Party and I didn't know where I stood in the Party anymore. I started to feel embarrassed that I had ever thought I was relevant to it at all. I might not have been a politician, a chief of staff, or even a senior staff member, but the Labor Party had become my whole identity. Despite such a strong sense of belonging in the beginning, I'd started to feel like belonging was for the people at the top, the people with power, who had earned their colleagues' and peers' respect. Not for someone who went on reality TV.

I think some of my staffer friends felt sorry for me. They knew I didn't really have any friends in Canberra other than those I'd made at work, so hearing I was home they invited me to Labor's end-of-session drinks at Hotel Realm, a Canberra institution. The drinks were to celebrate the conclusion of the first section of the sitting calendar and they were generally pretty rowdy. As soon as I walked in, I could feel I was the topic of conversation: I was the 'girl who had resigned from Bill Shorten's office to go on *The Bachelor*'. When I passed groups of people to go to the bar, or say hello to someone I knew, the volume would dip, only returning once I had gone.

As drinks were downed, the whispered conversations became louder. I'd managed enough Dutch courage to start sharing details of my six-week reality TV jaunt with former colleagues and friends. They responded with some of the nice reactions, presumably omitting the crueller appraisals of my decision.

I traded them a story about how the Honey Badger had taken a full bite straight out of a wheel of brie on one of his single dates, and we were soon all giggling. A warm feeling of acceptance washed over me once more.

It would have just clocked ten p.m. when I found myself in conversation with two members of Parliament and one of my favourite senior staff members from my old office. I was pretty trepidatious about sharing *Bachelor* gossip with actual members of Parliament but as we veered towards the subject I gave a self-deprecating performance about how it had been such a crazy decision and that I did in fact realise I may have just resigned from the office of the future prime minister. My former colleague piped up with some kind remarks about following my heart. I think he could sense my nerves as I took jabs at myself.

Despite having worked with politicians and in political offices for years, I was still not desensitised to socialising with them and I felt an intense mix of intimidation and admiration as we talked. I knew one of the MPs fairly well; he was in the Right faction like me and close to some Queenslanders I'd gone through student politics with. The other MP was a woman in the Left. I'd never met her before, but I knew she'd been around for a while. I also knew she was involved with Emily's List, a group in the Party that fundraised and mentored Labor women to help them get elected to Parliament. I was happy to be chatting with her—she'd always seemed like a good person to know.

I was halfway through a story about how I thought we should recruit Osher to run for the Party, when I noticed her swaying. She put down her wine glass, like she was almost trying to balance on it and then proceeded to tell me that *The Bachelor* was trash. It wasn't anything I hadn't heard before but I assumed she was joking and laughed along, until she lifted a hand to stop me. She said that I had degraded myself.

'You should be embarrassed,' she said.

I could feel myself freeze up. I looked at the other MP and my friendly colleague. They were equally taken aback. She didn't stop; she lectured me for a full five minutes, concluding by saying I was going to bring the Party into disrepute.

She'd just handed me all my deepest insecurities on a platter. So succinctly, so directly. I left the event not long after our conversation and spent the rest of the night sitting in front of my heater staring at my suitcases, which were only half unpacked. For the first time since resigning from my job, I really took stock of what I had done and what it meant. Her words suddenly gave the whispered judgements validity. I considered that maybe she was right. Maybe in seeking some easy fun, some short-term gratification, I'd thrown away an entire career. Maybe no one would take me seriously, I wouldn't have a place in the Party.

The MP's words swirled with Bobette's. Maybe I had made a mistake.

There were four months between the show filming and airing. I'd been eliminated from the show in late April and the show wasn't expected to air until August. I tried to stay in Canberra for as long as possible, but I felt increasingly alone so I started to escape at every opportunity. I spent some time in Queensland on my aunt's farm and a month in Bali with Cat, who had returned there after leaving the mansion. We spent our mornings exploring Canggu and afternoons parked up with Bintangs on the beach, trying the phone numbers of those we suspected were the top four girls, waiting to see if we'd get a dial tone. By the time promotional ads for the season began featuring on TV, I didn't feel like I could stay in Canberra at all and moved in with Hannah and James in Sydney temporarily to watch the whole thing play out.

One of the first ads focused on Vanessa Sunshine. Vanessa was blunt, opinionated and truly didn't give a fuck—in other words, a TV producer's dream. In the mansion, producers had quickly jumped on the quirk of her name and prompted her to introduce herself as Vanessa Sunshine, rather than simply

Vanessa. In the promo, the editors mashed up a succession of clips showing her introducing herself as instructed. My feature came in a ten-second talking head. 'Vanessa Sunshine has walked into this party,' I narrated as clips of Vanessa flashed on the screen, my voice dripping in sarcasm. 'And we know she's Vanessa Sunshine because she's told us fifteen times.'

I was on TV.

Messages from old schoolfriends and uni mates started to sprinkle in. *'Omg you're on The Bachelor?!', 'I just saw you on Channel Ten!!!'* I rode the high of the thirty-second ad spots littered through *MasterChef* all the way to 15 August 2018. Premiere night.

It was a Wednesday and I'd meticulously planned a party at Hannah and James' place, lovingly preparing a spread of hummus, crackers and cheese of every type. Friends streamed in with bottles of prosecco and the ground rules were set: no speaking except during ad breaks, although particularly incisive commentary on red-carpet arrivals would be permitted.

I pumped up the volume and shushed the persistent chatter in the room with a violent, flapping hand gesture as the first few girls started to step out of the limo. Everyone scattered around the living room was still bemused that I was going to be appearing on a reality TV show. To them, it was all a bit of a novelty. But I'd lived this.

I placed myself inches away from the TV set and analysed every choice made by post-production, dissecting every single limo exit.

'Was that girl really the first to meet Nick that night?'

'I wonder when they shot that introductory piece for her.'

'God, they're going hard on the wifey music for Brooke.'

My entrance was relegated to a montage of ten women somewhere in the middle of the episode—the part of the episode that people miss when they grab another bottle of champers from the fridge or do a quick wee. I'd already managed the expectations of my friends in the room, kicking off the night with iterations of 'Oh, I don't think I'll be featured much.' But still, when I saw myself flit across the TV in just a handful of seconds, a little twang of sadness crept up into my throat.

Thankfully, I was set to feature more significantly once we got to the cocktail party in the latter part of the episode. That was because while most of the girls had gotten back into their dresses to be interviewed about that night once, I'd done it twice.

Just after I'd been eliminated from the show, before I headed back to Canberra, I received a phone call from Marti, the executive producer. She asked if I was still in Sydney and whether I'd be happy to come back to the mansion to do a few more interviews. Of course I was happy to come back; I was elated.

It meant production trusted me, they liked me—I felt special. A production assistant picked me up the next day and sneaked me back onto set, into one of the demountables where they conducted our interviews.

On arrival, I learnt we'd be covering the premiere episode and I needed to be in my very first cocktail party dress—a structured, navy strapless gown, simple and elegant. I had tried on at least eight different dresses in the ten minutes each girl was allocated with wardrobe before filming commenced and I'd fallen in love with it right away. But the wardrobe department wasn't particularly prepared for my return and we were forced to improvise with a silky piece of navy fabric held around my torso with a bunch of pegs.

The first days in the mansion were as chaotic for production as they were for the girls. The producers were scrambling to establish storylines and figure out what would still matter in five or six episodes' time. They needed to get as much relevant commentary from the girls as possible at the time, so it could be spliced into something interesting down the track, because there were no second chances. That is, unless you have a very obliging contestant who's willing to come back in six weeks' time once you've settled on your plot.

In the interview chair, a producer briefed me on their intentions for the first episode. They told me they had clips of one of the girls, Cass, stalking Nick through the entire first cocktail party. I hadn't really noticed at the time—it was such a busy night—but I was determined to be helpful, so I colourfully commented on the scenes they described, once again buoyed by the producer's laughter. It hit the right note when it aired in the premiere. It was the perfect mix of cheekiness and shade, without edging too close to being a complete bitch.

I'd been careful to not go too hard, knowing that I didn't know exactly what I was narrating. Production most definitely had clips of Cass at the first cocktail party. In the episode, they interspersed my commentary with shots that appeared to show her staring at the Bachelor around corners or monitoring other girls' conversations with him. My interviews fit in seamlessly with the narrative the audience was being served up. By the end of the episode, Cass had been neatly packaged up as a 'stage five clinger', another favourite trope of the franchise.

After my friends departed into the night, I lay in bed, my room filled with soft light emanating from my phone as I flicked through articles, forums and anything else I could get my hands on. The reviews were glowing.

Someone called Michelle posted a picture of me in my improvised cocktail party dress, with the caption, 'Who is this girl? She's just spilling the tea with the producers and I am here for it.' The superfans in the forum labelled me the 'funny narrator'.

It was everything I had hoped for.

The week fast became dedicated to Channel Ten. On Thursday, I watched the next episode of *The Bachelor* go to air with Romy at her sister's apartment in Randwick. And on Sunday, I was due to attend the premiere party of a new Channel Ten pilot hosted by former federal Labor Senator Sam Dastyari. It was a panel talk show, unpacking the latest scandals and outrages across pop culture and politics, in the style of *Gruen* or *The Chaser*, cooler than *Q&A*, grittier than *The Project*. Sam was a political animal. He joined the Party when he was just sixteen, rose to the rank of general secretary by twenty-four and was a senator by thirty. But at thirty-five, he was suddenly out. He decided to resign from the Senate after a protracted controversy around his connections to Chinese political donors. I couldn't fathom working so hard, wanting something so much and finally getting where you'd always wanted to be, only to have it all disappear in a matter of months. But he was okay. Since resigning, he'd built a not-insignificant media career as an affable political commentator. He'd do spots on popular commercial radio shows, earning a reputation for stripping down the sterile veneer of politics, opting for gossip and banter instead.

I arrived later than I'd intended. Speeches had just wrapped and an up-tempo electronic beat pulsed through the room. The title credits rolled on the screen that had been set up against the back wall of the pub. White block text against a red background popped up, announcing the title of the show: 'Disgrace!'

I stretched onto my toes to get a better look over the crowd. The room was thronging with an eclectic mix of media personalities, politicians and staffers. In one corner was 'Intern Pete' from *The Kyle & Jackie O Show* and in the other was the top dog of the NSW Labor Party, General Secretary Kaila Murnain.

I was nervous; this was my first attempt at a Labor Party event since the end-of-session drinks I'd left, humiliated. The drinks where I'd been branded with the same label as Sam's show. But I took comfort in Sam's story. He'd made a mistake and here he was repackaging his pain into a zingy, thirty-minute special all of his own. If *The Bachelor* turned out to be mine, maybe there was still space for me too.

My eyes moved between the screen and the former senator. Sam was managing to do what I so desperately hoped to: he was bringing together two polarised worlds, simply because he loved them both. He loved being the ostentatious media personality and he loved the Labor Party.

The pilot was good. Sam's panel jumped into a range of controversial topics and disarmed the audience with self-reflexivity, nuance and humour. He was getting rave reviews on Twitter and when the episode wrapped, the party kicked off. I meandered around the room, smiling politely at people I knew by face but not by name. It was end-of-session drinks all over again. I was the girl who used to work for Bill Shorten who went on *The Bachelor*. I numbed my anxiety with three pints in quick succession as I stood on the periphery of groups and tried to laugh at the correct intervals. I was doing fine, but it didn't feel like it used to, when I worked for the Party. I wasn't in the fold anymore. I felt like an outsider.

Just as I was about to give up on the night, I found myself in a conversation with Kaila Murnain. Like Sam, Kaila was a political animal. She'd attended her first party conference at the age of fifteen and was elected NSW Labor's first female general secretary at the age of twenty-nine. I hadn't had much to do with Kaila; she was a boss and I was a baby by comparison, but I knew she was powerful and that she looked after people. She'd actually helped me get the job in Bill Shorten's office, like it was no big deal. She'd simply heard I was interested and put in a call. At that time, I'd been intoxicated by both her kindness and her power. But by the time she started chatting to me at Sam's party, I was actually just intoxicated.

Kaila was genuinely intrigued about *The Bachelor* and asked me all about it. Her questions felt different to the others I'd fielded that night. They weren't sprinkled with condescension or immediately followed by inquiries about my employment status. She was just curious about the whole thing. And thanks to the pints I'd sculled I happily volunteered anything and everything she wanted to know. In fact, I shared my full existential crisis: the sentences rolled out of my mouth and I couldn't stop them. I told her I was worried about my future, that I thought I had made a mistake, and that I feared I wouldn't be able to ever get a job again. She looked at me sympathetically and paused.

'Want a job?' she asked.

So simple. Three words and I was back. She really was a problem-solver. I was to come into Sussex Street, the headquarters of the NSW Labor Party, on Monday and she'd sort it all out, just like that. She gave me a hug and a kiss on the cheek, picked up her handbag and walked through the sparse crowd that remained. A blur of a blue blazer and clicking nude pumps. I looked back down at my beer and up to the exposed brick wall. For the first time in a long time, I felt anchored. Kaila made me feel like everything was going to be okay, like maybe I didn't have to feel stretched into two. She made me feel like I could exist entirely as myself, not just the girl who used to work for Bill Shorten and not just the girl who went on *The Bachelor*. I could just be Alisha with all the complexity that included.

I ordered an Uber and floated down the stairs to meet it. I had no clue what the job was and I didn't care. I was back in the Labor Party fold and that was all that mattered.

On Monday, I turned up to Sussex Street as instructed and Kaila sat down with me in her office. The back wall was brimming with every autobiography of a Labor parliamentarian ever written; a black leather lounge set and oversized desk filled the rest of the room. Kaila said they needed help with fundraising and events. Ideas spilled out of her at a mile a minute, and I scribbled them down as she spoke. She wanted to start with a fundraiser featuring former Prime Minister Julia Gillard. I piped up and said I knew her chief of staff, a man called Bruce. I'd met him during a very brief window working at Sky News as a rookie producer, helping prepare important people to be interviewed on air. 'Amazing! Call him!' she punctuated my interruption before continuing her tirade of thoughts about the event.

I really appreciated her enthusiasm. In a sea of uninspiring, spiritless messaging, Kaila's passion for the Party and its success was so refreshing. She made me excited about politics again.

I walked into my new office and logged straight into my emails, searching for Bruce's number.

Just as I thought that everything was lining up, at seven-thirty p.m. on Wednesday the next week, it all began to come crashing down. The next episode of *The Bachelor* was airing, and the show became increasingly explicit in its narratives. It had been building since the end of last week's episode, which had featured Romy on a date with Nick. They'd made pizza, drunk copious amounts of wine and they'd kissed. In fact, they'd kissed several times. But as we watched the date replay on-screen, we realised that none of the kisses had been included. We sat in silence in the ad break, until I interrupted with, 'Didn't you . . . ?'

She nodded.

As the episode started up again, a now very intoxicated Romy walked into the cocktail party telling the girls that they'd kissed. Without any footage of said kisses included, it made her look unhinged. The climax of the episode was Romy planting a very sloppy kiss on the neck of an unsuspecting Nick Cummins. It was awkward and uncomfortable. He was shown to reject her advances and in his accompanying interviews he said, 'She came in hot. Real hot.' Nick went on to say that he usually likes to hold back a bit and establish a real emotional connection with the person he's dating. Someone turned off the TV. Romy was already on the balcony taking a call from the Channel Ten publicist. I had reached for my phone and searched #TheBachelorAU hashtag to see the reaction live. One tweet called Romy a monster. Another, a predator.

Tonight, the tweets had started up again. This time they were about an equally awkward interaction between Cat and Nick during some one-on-one time. Feeling that her time with him wouldn't be considered a success if they didn't kiss, she'd asked him if he was 'tempted' to kiss her, to which he'd responded with a cringeworthy kiss on the cheek. The episode had ended with a heated argument at a cocktail party and, during the rose ceremony, Cayla, an energy healer from the Sunshine Coast, had labelled us snakes.

The show had found its focus. In the media, we were dubbed the mean girls and each episode brought more vitriol. I hadn't actually had all that much screentime, but we were a trio so I was guilty by association. My Instagram comments were flooded with sheep emojis. Cat's and Romy's were filled with people telling them what pieces of work they were and that their mothers must be proud.

The reaction of the girls from the show was mixed. Our relationships in real life weren't as starkly defined as they were on TV so a handful of them reached out to check whether we were okay. In fact, I'd caught up with Cayla a couple of months after filming. We'd had brekky and she'd even brought me a bag of Allen's lolly snakes, foreshadowing her on-screen interviews. Cayla messaged as the abuse poured in, but it felt like some of the girls happily leant into the dichotomy of bad and good.

By the time our elimination episode rolled around, we watched it together at Romy's place in a form of sad solidarity. Episode eight featured Cat's breakdown after Brooke received her second single date. We watched our conversation by the pool go to air, where Romy and I comforted her and she floated the idea of giving Nick an ultimatum. Once our conversation ended, instead of moving to another scene as the show generally did, production broke the fourth wall. Subtitles showed a producer asking us if our conversation was done and we watched as the crew moved away from their cameras, ostensibly packing up. But they had kept filming, and their cameras captured Romy asking Cat if she was going to cry when she spoke to Nick. 'Should I?' Cat responded. Romy encouraged her to do it, rounding off her advice with 'get to work, Cinderella'. It looked bad. It looked purposefully manipulative. But in reality it was less manipulative and more desperate. Cat felt rejected and had been grasping at straws; she wanted the Bachelor to understand that she was hurt, that she was relevant and worthwhile, before it was too late.

As the scene went to air, the texts and calls began. *'You fucking bitch. You're so fucking ugly, I'm surprised you were even cast,'* flashed up on Cat's phone. Then it began to ring. It was an unknown number but she answered anyway. Muffled abuse carried through the room. Cat hung up.

'Who the fuck was that?' I asked.

By now, we'd grown used to insults on Instagram. Both Cat and Romy had turned their comments off weeks ago. But this was Cat's personal phone number, and the calls were relentless. Her ringtone cut across the opening scenes of that night's toga-themed cocktail party. Another unknown number. Cat let it ring out, but they left a voicemail: 'How does it feel to have the entire country hate you? You're a fucking cunt of a thing.'

The phone fell silent as Romy and one of the girls who had recently received a single date, Tenille, argued on-screen. Tenille had previously called it 'gross' to kiss on a first date, but after her single date she'd come back to the mansion and provided a blow-by-blow account of her make-out sesh with the Bachelor to a room full of women who were halfway in love with the guy. It had not been well received and Romy had taken it upon herself to be the spokesperson for the house—of course lacking any tact after a couple of champagnes.

An ad break interrupted their back and forth and Cat's phone lit up again. Texts upon texts. Cat's iPhone blinked frantically, trying to keep up with the incoming messages.

'I hope you get hit by a bus.'

'You're the scum of the earth.'

The calls kept coming and in a panic we all agreed she should turn her phone off. *How had this happened?* The Instagram messages were one thing, but this was frightening. Romy messaged Channel Ten as I searched for an explanation. *She must be being doxxed*, I thought to myself. Someone's put her number up on Reddit or a shady Facebook group. In reality, the explanation was much simpler and less sinister: she still had her phone number displayed on her Instagram account, right next to the email button. Cat meekly turned her phone back on and removed it from her profile. We poured another glass of wine and sank into the couch.

The climax of the episode came in a conversation between the Bachelor and Tenille. He used a handful of tea lights on the table in front of him as props, labelling them Cat, Romy and Alisha. 'Who is being mean?' he asked Tenille. She pushed all the candles towards him. By the end of the episode, all three 'mean girls' had left the mansion.

Viewers rejoiced online, but there was little to celebrate at Romy's house. A lonely cork from a bottle of Yellowtail rested next to a sad smear of quince paste. Osher's voice announcing the preview of the next episode bounced sombrely throughout the house. Few words were exchanged between us. Romy was frantically texting her sisters and Cat looked blankly towards the repeat of *FBI* that was now playing on the TV.

I reached for my iPhone to order an Uber. With two despondent hugs, I left Romy's apartment, moving my weight from foot to foot as I waited and the cold Sydney air bit my shoulders. Twenty minutes later I was home and I lay in bed, fixated on my phone, reading recap after recap that neatly packaged how detestable we all were.

Unlike Cat and Romy, I left my comments on. I wasn't exactly sure why.

It was complex.

There was a part of me that felt we needed to be held accountable. In the wash-up of the season, it was clear there were many things we'd done that we'd regret. I thought about my post-elimination interview and my comments about Cass, ironically, one of the very few moments I'd been celebrated by the audience. It didn't deserve celebration. It was shitty. I'd wanted production's approval so desperately that I'd happily helped them write the first chapter of their story, with little regard for its accuracy. I reflected on edgy jokes I'd thought were funny and the snide sidebar comments we'd made, glued together as three. I consumed the comments as a form of self-flagellation, like maybe if I read enough of them I would be absolved of my sins.

'I'm so fucking happy you three cunts were eliminated'

'Just as ugly on the inside as you are on the outside, pure evil you are'

'Pathetic little troublemaker'

There was a part of me that just wanted to matter. When Channel Ten had ferried Cat, Romy and I around Sydney the day after our elimination to do media, I'd been relegated to the sidelines of a number of interviews. I hadn't been a villainous enough villain, not awful enough to be relevant. I'd been forgotten. The comments, even as they eviscerated me, made me feel like I existed.

'Bitch'

'Sheep'

'Trailer park'

There was a part of me, the biggest part, that desperately cared what people thought of me. It's why I spent hours after each episode reading every comment I could get my hands on. It's why I kept returning to the forums for *Bachelor* superfans and had grown so fixated on the opinions of one of the users in particular—Bobette. I didn't understand people who could move through the world not giving a fuck. I gave so many fucks. I think, at the heart of it, that's why I applied for the show in the first place. I wanted affirmation that I was a good person, a worthwhile person. Someone that people would care about and would want to know. The affirmation wasn't enough from my friends, from my family or from my mum, who had poured love all over me. My mind wouldn't recognise it. I needed a bigger sample size and it was as if I felt like the response to a national TV show would be more empirical. I couldn't just not read the comments. That was my data.

I got into the habit of replying to the comments and to the messages that flooded my Instagram inbox. I even went on a date with one of the senders, Lachlan from Bondi. The night my elimination episode aired, he messaged that if I'd spent less time 'sucking off' Cat and Romy, the Bachelor might have been interested in me. I can't tell you why that opener led to my flirtatious reply, but I can tell you that two weeks later I was kissing him on Liverpool Street in the CBD after a few too many pints at The Sydney Cidery in World Square.

I also messaged Melissa Mason, a journalist at PEDESTRIAN. TV, who had described me as Cat and Romy's sad little henchman. *'Oh man, your ranking article is brutal,'* I said, adding a laughing emoji in the hope she'd think I was nice and casual and didn't take myself too seriously. Her reply matched my energy, saying she liked to think that she was ranking us as characters painted by producers, rather than ripping us to shreds personally.

These little interactions made me feel like I was clawing back some control of the narrative against the swelling tide of hate. Australia en masse might loathe me on-screen, but one on one, in conversation, I felt I could get people to see a fuller picture.

I had just wanted people to like me. I'd always wanted to be liked.

It was why I'd opted for Alicia over Alisha and why I'd lied about being a star athlete. I didn't seem to trust that who I was would be good enough, so I began to embellish. In Year 3 the cool girls in our grade remarked that I looked like the young blonde girl in the latest Uncle Toby's ad on TV. So, of course, wanting their attention and admiration, I lied and said that it was me and I'd been on a real TV set with big cameras, lots of lights and had even had my own room with my name on the door. What I hadn't realised was that the girls were very well aware it wasn't me; they were baiting me, and for the rest of the school year they taunted me, asking about minuscule details of the advertisement. What was the actor like that played my dad? Where did I shoot it? How much was I paid?

Then there was the time in Year 4 I tried to lie about breaking my leg when I noticed how much attention kids with a cast received. As their bone healed over the course of weeks, every inch of their cast would fill with signatures and drawings scratched across the fibreglass. I wanted those signatures so badly that I hurled myself off a small flight of stairs, and screamed and cried until the school sent me off to Royal North Shore Hospital, where I somehow conned my way into a series of X-rays. They confirmed that my leg was not in fact broken.

And there was the time in Year 5, when I had such a huge crush on a Year 6 boy at a vacation care I attended while Mum worked. He let me ride on his bike pegs and told me I was a good singer when I did Atomic Kitten's 'Tide is High' for karaoke. I told him I was in Year 6 too but was soon racked with guilt and was convinced he'd find out. I pleaded with Mum to not send me back, to send me anywhere else, so fearful was I that he would discover who I really was.

'Cow'

'BULLY'

'Cunt'

I couldn't reply fast enough to the comments to make any material impact.

A week after our elimination episode aired, Brooke came to stay with me in Sydney. She was still on the show; she'd made it to the top four. Channel Ten was pushing out previews about a 'big secret' she would soon reveal to the Bachelor, the secret being that she'd previously had relationships with women. She had been flown over from Perth in preparation for a string of media appearances.

Brooke had absolutely blown up as the series had aired. The audience had really connected with her and her story. The show foregrounded her vulnerability and authentic connection with Nick, and Australia saw her as the kind, compassionate person that she is. The night she arrived, I poured us two glasses of red wine and we talked through all the craziness that had transpired since the show began. We chatted about the red carpet, her single dates and the fact that over 10,000 people had followed her on Instagram during just the first episode. She had other news too. She'd been contacted by Warner Brothers about doing another show, *Bachelor in Paradise*. It was a relatively new spin-off of the main franchise; one season had been broadcast in Australia and it had only finished airing a couple of months ago. I'd watched it and I'd loved it. The show took rejects from previous seasons of *The Bachelor* and *The Bachelorette*, chucked them in a resort in Fiji and crossed their fingers they would fall in love.

'Are you going to do it?' I asked. She wasn't sure, she hadn't watched much of it. I forced her to watch some clips on her laptop, pointing out the free cocktails and the array of good-looking people. I'd also become a frequent lurker on the *Bachelor* forums and had read rumours that a former *Bachelor* winner, Alex Nation, had been approached by production for the next season. I knew Brooke thought she was hot, so pitched that as an idea too.

Once we'd comprehensively unpacked the proposition, Brooke jumped into the shower and I retrieved the bottle of wine from the kitchen. As I leant over to top up both our glasses, I noticed Brooke's emails, left open on the laptop. There were so many unopened messages. I couldn't help but stickybeak. Email after email: invitations to events, interview requests, even an offer to create her own activewear line. I was stunned. It was everything I had expected to come from a reality TV appearance; I just hadn't realised that it was actually happening for someone else because it was so far removed from my reality.

For us, there were no invitations, no collaborations. Even the hate mail eventually dissipated. I cringe now, thinking back, but I'd assumed that once you went on reality TV, you would be ever after followed by paparazzi, recognised by the general public and invited to glamorous events for which celebrity stylists wanted to dress you. Instead, the day before Brooke arrived, Romy, Cat and I found ourselves sitting on the verandah of a pub in Surry

Hills, investigating ways to anonymously message the phone number of a *Daily Mail* photographer that Romy had gotten her hands on. We'd assumed that when we all caught up for a drink in public, paparazzi would somehow just appear from thin air, hunting for a coveted picture of the villains of *The Bachelor* season six. When this didn't eventuate, we pondered the reality TV ecosystem over some salt and pepper squid.

'You know, people arrange those pictures with paparazzi,' Romy informed me.

I hadn't given it much thought, but it made sense. Why on Earth, across all of Sydney, would a photographer just happen to be in the exact spot, at the exact time, that two reality TV contestants shared a risqué kiss? It did seem quite coincidental.

'I've got a pap's number,' she continued.

If everyone was doing it, then why shouldn't we? The only problem was we were too embarrassed to send the text from our phones, which cued me downloading several apps that claimed they would anonymise my phone number. We workshopped what the text should say. *'Spotted. Bachelor villains. Cat, Romy and Alisha drinking at the Clock Hotel in Surry Hills.'*

Was it too long? Would they know it was from us? *Surely not*, I thought. Paps must receive tip-offs all the time. We sent the message and not long after my phone buzzed back at me.

A reply from the pap. *'Who is this?'*

We quickly sculled our drinks and moved on to a bar in the next suburb, too embarrassed to stay.

I couldn't help but envy Brooke and everything she was experiencing. I envied the emails, the followers, and the fact that she'd been warmly embraced by the audience. But most of all I envied her invitation from Warner Brothers to do another show.

My envy might not have made logical sense. The public reaction had been so vitriolic that I'd just been surviving day by day. I'd seen the hand of production. The way it could shape a contestant's story and by extension their destiny. I'd experienced its particularly powerful effect as someone that struggled to be self-assured. And I was back working for Labor, I was settled, back in the fold, when I'd feared I'd be alienated forever. Yet, I didn't want the *Bachelor* chapter to be over. Despite the experience resulting in basically nothing I had hoped, I'd loved filming and I loved the friendships that I'd made. And another show meant another opportunity. For Brooke, that might have meant a holiday, the opportunity to meet someone, or the ability to propel her public profile to even more wondrous heights. For me, it was a second chance. A second chance to show the world who I thought I was. It had been their stage that had led to my current reception. Maybe going back could be my chance at redemption.

The call came, but it couldn't have come at a worse time. I was on the phone to Julia Gillard's chief of staff, trying to bed down her flights for our fundraiser. It was planned for November 2018, just two months away. As soon as I moved my handset from my face and saw the string of numbers, I just knew it was Warner Brothers. I quickly told Bruce I'd call him back. I was right, it was a casting assistant called Tam. She could hardly get her words out before I was shouting my interest down the phone. She laughed, attempting to slow me down. 'This is just an initial call,' she said. 'There are no guarantees.' She said she'd send over a questionnaire for me to fill out, which she needed back by Thursday. They were still in the phase of deciding the cast and were figuring out how everyone would fit. I thanked Tam profusely, hoping my politeness would somehow take me one step further to securing a spot. Before I rang Bruce back, I messaged Cat. *Have you gotten a call for BIP?*

She had. Romy had as well. They'd decided not to tell me in case my call never came. Cat was excited about the offer for similar reasons to my own, but she told me Romy was less so. She had very little trust in Warner Brothers and she'd felt manipulated by the Channel Ten publicity team—she thought they'd given us bad advice in regard to dealing with the media. Advice that served to solidify our character archetype, rather than help humanise us. Cat said she was considering her options.

I was that invested in going back, I discussed it with Kaila after the first call. It was an eerily similar conversation to the one I'd had eight months earlier, with Bill Shorten's chief of staff. I explained to her that I'd been approached and again pitched the idea of leave without pay. Again, I spoke fast, apologising that I hadn't been with the team for long and assuring her I'd sell 300 tickets to our Julia Gillard fundraiser before I left. She laughed. This time, the response was different. 'Of course, you're going,' she said. 'The Party will still be here in a month.' I would've kissed her on the mouth if I didn't think that then I'd definitely have to resign.

I sent the questionnaire in by Wednesday afternoon. By Thursday, I'd found out that Romy had officially declined the offer. I became worried when she decided not to do it. I thought that without her, Warner Brothers wouldn't be interested in me. I was only as good as whatever the hook was. It was meant to be a reunion of the mean girls, and what was the point of Gretchen and Karen without Regina? I felt embarrassed that I'd already spoken to Kaila and told a handful of my friends. Even more so, I was mortified that last night I'd celebrated with half a bottle of flat champers I'd found in the fridge and then sent a bunch of emails to various Australian fashion brands hinting that I was about to be on another show, wondering if they wanted to 'collaborate'. It was the paparazzi text message all over again. How desperate.

I spent the next few weeks on edge, waiting for the phone to ring, waiting for Warner Brothers to tell me I'd been cut. Of course, they wouldn't like me for just me. People only liked me in relation to something or someone else. Because I had a cool cast and a pair of crutches. Because I was in an Uncle Toby's ad. Because I worked for Bill Shorten. Because I was market-able as a mean girl.

I didn't allow myself to feel secure until I was sitting on the plane to Nadi Airport. Not when I passed my second medical, not when the Travel and Talent Manager sent me my flight details and not even when Sam Dastyari messaged saying his producer friend from Channel Ten had confirmed I'd been cast. But the days crept forward, and the phone didn't ring. It didn't ring as I packed my bags. It didn't ring as I scrolled my camera roll, searching for pictures to send Hannah to keep my Instagram active. And it didn't ring as I boarded flight VA181: Sydney to Paradise.

CHAPTER 5

Paradise

'Paradise' was, in actuality, one of the more budget accommodation options in Fiji. Ordinarily it would be home to backpackers and big family groups, but every November it was transformed into a television set.

Before we entered the set, we were sequestered, just like before *The Bachelor*, but this time at a hotel ten minutes away called the Naviti. Three days with another cast member and a minder in two adjoining hotel rooms. No phones, no internet.

While we were sequestered, Warner Brothers' art department headed into *Paradise* and lovingly cable-tied buckets of fake frangipanis to the trees. They shipped over massive pieces of foam upholstered in tropical prints to liven up the beige bungalows around the pool, and threaded huge rattan lanterns between palm trees. The setting was already idyllic but the added hibiscus flowers really made *Paradise* pop—even if they were plastic.

I was sequestered with Cat. We were so excited to have been asked back for a second season and both saw it as a vehicle to redeem ourselves in the eyes of the audience. From what we'd seen of the first season, *Bachelor in Paradise* seemed to provide a better opportunity than *The Bachelor* to share a more well-rounded view of ourselves. There was more time spent on each contestant, the structure of the show was more relaxed and the representations seemed more complex.

I had been checking the forums religiously before we left and informed Cat that Bobette was almost certain she would be appearing. Cat didn't seem to care about the forums, but she always appreciated my intel. We spent the long, drawn-out days of the sequester doing half-baked workouts on the concrete tiles in our hotel room and speculating about who we thought might also have been cast. Thankfully this time we had a TV, so when we weren't trying to work off the room-service menu of pizza and pasta, we were flicking through seemingly endless Fijian TV channels trying to find something in English. We watched so many episodes of *Robot Wars* in seventy-two hours we could practically have engineered a robot ourselves.

In the final rounds of casting for *Bachelor in Paradise*, we were asked who we most wanted to meet out of every season of *The Bachelor* in Australia. Producers called it our wish list. Cat wanted to meet Richie Strahan. Richie had been the third lead of the franchise, and personally, I doubted he'd be there. A former lead of the franchise had never appeared on *Bachelor in Paradise*—not even in America, which was up to its fifth season of the spin-off.

I had written down Paddy, the villain in the most recent season of *The Bachelorette*. He was known for describing the Bachelorette as 'fit as fuck' and juggling a soccer ball down the red carpet to meet her. He had a thick Manc accent, platinum blond hair and wore pants two sizes too small. I didn't think he'd been too bad on the show: he was arrogant, sure, but mostly cheeky and harmless. Given my recent experience with being cast as the villain, I decided there might be more to him than his portrayal on the show and I was certain production wouldn't miss a chance to offer him round two in Fiji.

In fact, I had messaged him after an episode aired that painted him as particularly obnoxious, in an attempt to pre-game. It was quite common for people to try to pre-game *Paradise*. People wanted to stay around as long as possible—for both the pay cheque and the free pina coladas—so they'd try to set up relationships, or at the very least friendly alliances, before flying out to ensure they had someone to keep them around during the rose ceremonies, which operated in a similar way to the main show. In *Bachelor in Paradise*, the producers ensured there was an uneven number of men and women at any one time and staggered new arrivals throughout the season so that when a rose ceremony was held, a handful of either men or women would be sent home.

Paddy hadn't been particularly receptive to my flirtation, and I'd been far too nervous to collude in any sort of concrete way. I wasn't sure how explicit about this stuff other cast members were, so I'd chickened out before going too deep.

On the third morning of our sequester, a white slip of paper appeared underneath our door: 'Cat 11.30 a.m. Alisha 2 p.m. Be in full hair and make-up, ready to shoot.' Today was the day. Cat jumped into the shower. I kneeled on a chair over the bathroom sink to apply a face mask that claimed to detoxify, brighten and tighten.

Talking over the noise of the shower, we contemplated what this whole new thing would bring. What I loved about Cat was that in stark contrast to her portrayal as the brash, manipulative mean girl, she was in reality sensitive and self-deprecating. More than anything, Cat just wanted to meet someone. She wanted someone to embrace her, all of her. To be into all her quirks, all her 'too muchness'.

It was hard to fully give yourself over to the fantasy of meeting someone on *The Bachelor*. I'd tried my utmost but I was also realistic. There were just too many barriers to that happening: the number of women you're competing against, the environment you're expected to connect in and the slim shot of actually being compatible with the Bachelor himself. But *Bachelor in Paradise* was an entirely different format, and the first season of the show had ended with three couples declaring their love for one another. These were much better odds, so we allowed ourselves to dream.

'I can't believe Sam and Tara broke up,' I projected over the sound of the water.

'Did they?' Cat replied. She was never up with the gossip.

'Babe, they looked so in love on the show. It looked so real,' I said.

I had been obsessed with Sam and Tara, a couple who had gotten engaged on the last season. It had looked real; it'd looked like a fairytale, like they just really connected. The whole season had basically been set around their love story. But just two months after the finale aired, they had revealed that they'd split. Not only had they split but they had detailed in various news outlets just how toxic their relationship had been. The sparkly, romantic music had worked on me and I'd wanted to believe everything was as simple as it seemed.

'As long as there's someone who can actually hold a conversation, it'll be good enough for me,' Cat replied.

Cat left at her allocated time, and then it was my turn. On set, the camera crew shot a variety of takes of me walking along a sandy, winding path and pushing open the doors to 'Paradise'. Before I could continue through the doors and down the path, a voice would yell 'thanks!' and 'repo' and we would repeat it all again. It wasn't until a good hour later, with a drone hovering overhead, that I was cued to continue walking into the resort to meet my fellow castmates.

The experience of *Bachelor in Paradise* was completely unlike *The Bachelor*. Where the latter was tightly managed, with producers controlling the beats of the show like a conductor with their orchestra, *Bachelor in Paradise* was loose and spontaneous, with crew scurrying around the set trying to keep on top of the evolving relationships and emerging conflicts. *Paradise* was shot much more in the style of *Big Brother*, with cameras rolling from ten a.m. until late into the night. The bar opened at midday and we were allowed two drinks an hour, which culminated in a significant buzz as the afternoon bled into the evening.

A large group was already gathered around the bar when I entered, but I was apprehensive about talking to them. I had grown so accustomed to the conventions of the previous show that it felt like I would be breaking the rules. Once I'd done a round of introductions, I sidled up to a producer off to one side and asked if I was allowed to just stand and talk with the group. They laughed. 'Of course you are,' they said, gesturing for me to go and mingle.

There were plenty of familiar faces. Brooke was already there, along with a handful of other girls from the Honey Badger's season: Brittney Weldon, who had captured Australia's hearts by trying to start a conga line at a cocktail party, and Cass Wood, who I'd famously called a bunny boiler as I narrated her interest in Nick. The environment at the bar was incredibly overwhelming, with loud voices projecting over louder voices. My body was pumping so much adrenaline I was practically tingling.

Cat slipped into the space beside me and nudged me in the ribs. 'Look!' she said, in excited disbelief.

Paddy had just walked in and was making a beeline for the bar. I suddenly went red, knowing I'd have to deal with the consequences of my cringeworthy advances. Paddy's accent carried as he bantered with the boys from his season. I decided to rip the bandaid off and greet him, expecting some sort of reaction, maybe a wink or a knowing nod. Instead, Paddy leant in and grabbed my right shoulder in a hug like we were bro-ing down. 'And what's your name?' he asked as he released me. *Fuck*, I thought. *He has no clue who I am.*

Cat and I escaped to our new room on the set for an emergency debrief. We were staying in traditional Fijian wood-and-straw huts called bures, containing two single beds framed in mosquito nets. I sat on the one closest to the door, mortified by how many horny fire reacts I'd sent in response to his Instagram stories.

Cat dismissed my worries immediately, telling me it was totally fine. I should go strike up a conversation with Paddy and then let the producers know I was into him. Then she pivoted the conversation to how hot Richie Strahan was. I actually hadn't even registered him in the crowd; I'd been too overwhelmed by my own embarrassment. I didn't know how she could be so relaxed, so immediately comfortable in this new environment. I decided I was going to try to emulate her confidence. I no longer wanted to be a side character in my own story. I left the bure and made a beeline for the nearest producer, registering my interest.

Paddy and I turned out to be one of the early success stories of our season of *Paradise*. In the first few days of shooting, producers urged me to set up a cute date for him, during which I had my first on-camera kiss and Paddy called me 'fit as fuck', which really ticked all my reality TV fan boxes. After the standard *Bachelor* cheeseboard and wine, we went for a sunset paddleboard and talked about his relationship with his family, particularly how close he was with his sister, before heading back into the bay to get ready for our first rose ceremony.

There were more girls than boys, meaning the boys would have the power. Two girls would be going home. Heading into the first cocktail party, which preceded the elimination, Paddy and I realised that surprisingly we were the strongest couple. Everyone else was scrambling, trying to secure their ticket to stay, while Paddy and I sat at the bar, drinking cocktails and playing the part of boyfriend and girlfriend. Cat had been quietly confident going into the cocktail party. While I had busied myself with Paddy, she said she'd been connecting with Richie and felt fairly certain she'd receive his rose.

During the rose ceremony, Osher called out the boys' names one by one and they stepped up to a mark set by production and named the girl they wanted to give their rose to. One by one, they said names that weren't Cat's. Richie was second to last. He gave his rose to Cass. The only person left with a rose that hadn't been promised was a guy called Nathan, who stepped forward and gave his rose to Brittney.

What was meant to be Cat's redemption had turned into another chapter of rejection. 'Fuck this,' she said, turning and running from the rose ceremony set.

I followed her back into the bar area, trying to ignore the cameras following us. I encouraged her into the toilet, where I knew we could be heard but not seen. Her body crumpled against the door in a ball. She thought it was a set-up, that the producers had brought her all this way to elicit these exact emotions. She felt that they knew she would be rejected, that nobody in the cast would want to connect with someone who had already been branded a villain. Heavy tears fell from her eyes, staining her white linen jumpsuit with mascara.

'I just don't get it,' she said between sobs. 'I'm trying to be so genuine and trying to meet someone, and I don't understand why people don't like me.'

We sat on the tiled floor for twenty minutes. In a way it did feel like a trick, like this had been the first frame on a storyboard on some whiteboard in some room we couldn't enter. When Cat left, I wondered where my name might be on that whiteboard, whether my story had already been written.

Less than twelve hours later, Paddy ended it with me, saying that I'd shown my true colours in supporting Cat. I feared he'd just sealed my fate. I was set for another season affirming my badness.

That was until the resort received a slew of new faces.

The first new arrival was Davey Lloyd. He'd been a fan favourite on the first season of *The Bachelorette* and had returned for the first season of *Bachelor in Paradise*. The other would completely reshape my *Bachelor* experience. His name was Jules Bourne.

Jules was twenty-four and from Kiama on the NSW South Coast. I knew him from his season of *The Bachelorette*, although it hadn't quite finished airing by the time we flew to Fiji. He'd walked into the mansion in a blazer adorned with medals. He had shared with Bachelorette Ali Oetjen that he was a former infantry officer who had served in Afghanistan. During his time on the show, he became famous for his extremely animated reactions during rose ceremonies, showing the Bachelorette a tattoo of his best friend's band on his left butt cheek and sharing the fact that he'd never had a girlfriend.

When he walked into *Paradise*, I was drawn to him immediately. With one relationship already under my belt, I no longer dreaded 'pulling someone for a chat', so we ended up talking under one of the cabanas next to the pool and hit it off right away. Jules was an internet kid like me and for some reason our first conversation ended up navigating the vast terrain of Reddit, RuneScape and multi-level marketing. I felt like he was very much my speed and my intellectual equal.

We swapped all the superficial stories. I brought up the band tattoo and he told me about his best friend Jimmy Vann and his band The Vanns. I mentioned Hannah and said she probably knew of them, because she liked much cooler music than me.

Then we shared some deeper truths. He told me how much he loved the ocean and he touched my fingertips to his right shin where it'd snapped in a huge wave. When I pressed, I felt metal. He moved my fingers down his leg, finding one of the screws underneath his skin. These days he took photos of waves, finding calm in the moment as they curled.

For his waves, I traded him fire, telling him about the big bonfires my family would light on my aunt's farm in Caboolture. I could sit for hours, staring into the centre, watching the flames lick and dance.

I didn't want the conversation to end, but Davey came over with a date card. Since the women had the power at the next rose ceremony and I was currently the least attached, he announced that he had decided to take his chance with me.

You really couldn't have put more opposite people together. I was a big nerd and Davey was a cool guy from Sydney's Northern Beaches. Our conversation was formal and stilted. I was more flirtatious with the camera operator. Production quickly noticed how uptight I was and how many times I'd inadvertently mentioned Jules, so I was taken aside for a pep talk. The executive producer held me by my shoulders and implored me to loosen up, to just go with it, 'have some fun'. Minutes later, Davey went in for a kiss over our cheeseboard and, having been primed by production, I went along for the ride. The kiss was fine, and he was lovely, but I told him I felt we were more platonic. Davey looked confused and asked me what that meant.

Our kiss never made the final cut; I guess the producers thought it might prevent Barry from Broadmeadows calling me a slut on Facebook. I left the date with a new friend and a new-found appreciation for the persuasive power of producers.

I hightailed it straight back to Jules. I just wanted to be around him. We went to the bar to get some beers and took ourselves over to one of the day beds on set. I couldn't tell if the energy between us was mutual or I was just feeling a buzz from the alcohol. I told him everything about the date, including the kiss, ensuring I was explicit that I didn't like Davey in that way. I told him all I could think about was him, that I knew I was being direct and this was all happening very fast.

'This is all new to me too,' he assured me, shifting his weight on the pillows of the day bed and bringing our bodies closer together. We laughed at the intimacy of the scene and then suddenly we were sharing a kiss, only interrupted by someone yelling that another date card had arrived. This date card was for Jules and he chose to take me.

My head was spinning. In one day I'd been dumped, courted by Davey, kissed by Jules and was about to go on a second date. I'd hardly been noticed on *The Bachelor*, so I couldn't quite believe that this was all happening.

Jules and I were escorted to a separate part of the resort and met by a waiter, who told us we'd be tasting a series of aphrodisiacs. First asparagus, then oysters, with strawberries to finish. It was a truly excellent set-up by production: with the wrong couple you'd overlay the date with awkward music. But we completely embraced it. With each course, we egged on the other to be sillier and more outrageous. The result was more double-entendres than an Australian audience had ever seen.

'Close your eyes and open your mouth,' Jules whispered as he picked up an oyster.

'I've heard that one before,' I volleyed back as he tried to force-feed me. 'At least let me look civil with a fork,' I protested.

'Sometimes you've just got to finger the oyster,' he insisted, trying to flick the thing into the back of my throat.

The whole thing was disgusting and hilarious.

Clips from the interviews that we'd do later were inserted among footage from the last course of melted chocolate and strawberries. Jules told the camera it was the best date he'd ever been on. I told the camera the date was everything that I had been hoping it would be.

The date wrapped with a final glass of champagne and a discussion of rose ceremony politics. He told me that he hated it when men grovelled for a rose. He just wanted to talk to the person he was connecting with the most. Against the backdrop of a franchise so famous for artifice, we assured each other that what we were experiencing was genuine.

And the first time, I felt as if the cameras completely faded away and we were just two people on a date, having fun and enjoying each other's company. After years of failed high-school and university relationships, I'd always told myself to hold out for someone I really connected with. I was looking for a connection that felt easy and magnetic. The type of connection that I had with my girlfriends, where the conversation just flowed and the foundation was fun and friendship. On this first date with Jules, it felt like I'd found just that.

The next day, we went on another date, equally as enjoyable. There was the requisite cheeseboard and champagne, and he'd brought me my own party shirt, so I could match his eccentric style. I asked him how he was finding *Paradise*, to which he replied, 'Surprisingly easy. I'm having the best time.' Then we delved into our love lives, with Jules joking about what an eligible bachelor he was. 'I'm a catch, aren't I? Living with

my parents, never had a girlfriend and got a cat called Yogi.'
I interrogated the girlfriend part, asking whether he'd really
never had one. For someone who had never had a girlfriend, he
had some strong romantic instincts. He mentioned a couple of
names, a couple of past connections, but quickly pivoted back
to our date, pulling me towards him for a kiss. The whole thing
felt electric.

That night I lay in bed, going over every single detail of the
last two days and every single detail of the dates. I was absolutely wired with excitement about what was to come. My mind
jumped ahead to the commitment ceremony and what Bobette's
comments in the forum would be. *We were the Sam and Tara
of the season*, I thought to myself. It was happening.

My fantasy didn't last long. The next day we had a new arrival:
Tenille. The same Tenille who had told Nick Cummins six
months earlier that I was a bad person. Tenille made an instant
impact on the men in *Paradise*. She was tall, slim and beautiful.
I felt like a blob of plasticine beside her. One of our castmates,
Ivan, described her as a goddess, and almost immediately I felt
Jules' attention shift. He was transfixed. He called her a 'gypsy,
boho babe from Byron'. She was at the top of his wish list.

Tenille and I had a little reunion under a cabana; we were both quick to exchange apologies after the fallout from our season. Conflict on the show was never as deep or permanent as it may have seemed to a viewer. People are hard to hate close up. Jules joined our reconciliation and Tenille asked us about the lay of the land as the sun set. She wanted clarity about who was coupled up and who was still exploring things.

Jules took the liberty of answering for both of us. 'The reason we, sort of, don't want to tell you that is that it could influence you. You should just listen to this guy,' he said, gesturing his hand towards her heart. 'Go with what feels right and just vibe your way around *Paradise*.'

Tenille told him she didn't want to be Mrs Steal Your Man.

'No,' Jules replied, touching the back of her hand with his palm. 'But you still have to look after you.'

I stared at Tenille, my face contorted, trying to hide my discomfort.

Minutes later, Jules took Tenille by the hand and led her away for a private chat. In the course of one afternoon, with the arrival of one beautiful woman, everything had shifted and I didn't understand why.

For two full days, Jules avoided me. When I was having breakfast, he was having a shower. When I was at the bar, he was stand-up paddleboarding. When I sat by the pool, he stood by the beach, staring pensively out at the waves, while a nearby camera zoomed into his profile. I was being ghosted, but instead of receiving increasingly monosyllabic text messages, I had the pleasure of experiencing it in person.

In his private interviews with producers, Jules unpacked his inner turmoil. He told the producers that 'exploring a connection with one girl was new to him, let alone two', and he labelled his attraction to Tenille so 'weird and sparkly' that he felt compelled to pursue it.

In our rare interactions, he told me that he was 'aware' of the 'situation' and was 'working towards a solution'. There was something so deeply frustrating about not getting a straight answer. Had he been on the same dates as me?

Logically, I knew we had only known each other for a matter of days, but it had seemed so effortless and authentic. It made the speed at which he'd cast me aside all the more jarring.

Finally, after a good forty-eight hours—and several appeals from our castmates—Jules sat with me at the bar.

'Enough pensive staring, Jules,' I laughed at him. 'You've been pensively staring for days.'

He gave me the straight answer I'd been looking for. His exact words were, 'in terms of, like, me wanting to emotionally pursue you, I'm electing to not'. The delivery might have been jumbled but the message was clear.

I thought I could handle the conversation, I thought that clarity was what I wanted, but his answer cut me like a knife. There was part of me that knew this was where it was going to land the moment Tenille had walked in, but I desperately didn't want it to be true. I liked him so much. I didn't understand why he didn't like me too. I ended the conversation bitterly, my biting words masking my pain. I sarcastically wished him all the luck in the world before instructing the omnipresent producers to send in a new guy.

'Cue him,' I joked, looking out to the entry.

And they delivered: a guy called Wes, who looked like Aquaman's equally attractive brother, walked in moments later. Post-production scored the scene with some upbeat music in the final edit.

At the rose ceremony that same day the women had the power and two men were set to go home. During the cocktail party, I announced loudly to anyone who would listen that Jules would not be receiving my rose. Why would he? After days of me seeking clarity, he'd more than given me my answer, but me directing my rose elsewhere would mean that Jules would be going home. Tenille wasn't interested in him; she had started up a little something with our castmate Ivan. Jules came to talk to me during the cocktail party and it felt like a goodbye. I told him that if I was to have any self-respect, I needed to give my rose to somebody else.

I returned to my bure resolute. I wasn't giving Jules my rose. I sat on the edge of the bed and said as much to Alex Nation, who'd become my new roommate after Cat had left the show. In the corner of our room was a camera, called a hot head, which was remotely controlled by producers. In my peripheral vision I noticed the camera move to capture our conversation.

The executive producer from Warner Brothers walked into our room moments later. Marti had also been the EP on my first season of *The Bachelor*, but she'd been so high up in the production hierarchy that we'd barely seen more of her than the occasional quick briefing at the top of a rose ceremony, telling us to stand as still as we could so the whole thing would take the least amount of time possible. Marti wasn't the cut-throat, manipulative and ruthless person that you might imagine a high-flying TV producer to be. Well, she may in fact have been all of those things, but when you interacted with her she was tender and kind. She treated you as a mother would. I had gone into the toilet when I noticed the camera reposition, and was sitting on the lid. Marti walked into the small space and knelt down in front of me, opening the conversation gently.

She asked me how I was feeling but it was just small talk before pivoting to her main appeal: to consider keeping Jules around.

'Just to see what happens,' she said, making sure to remind me that I didn't have a meaningful connection with any other man. I pushed back, telling her that wasn't the point. The point was to move on. Yes, Jules would not receive a rose as a consequence, but that was not my concern. Marti was persistent but I wouldn't budge. I told her again, I was not going to do it.

Though, this time, exasperated, I added, 'If you can get him to do something, I might consider it.'

Marti had found her opening. She left our bure with a new task in hand, no doubt heading directly to Jules to make some magic happen.

Standing in the rose ceremony, I continued to war-game the various decisions in my head. If I gave my rose to Jules, I would look pathetic. But he would still be here, which would make my heart happy. If I gave my rose to somebody else, I would have my girl-power moment, but Jules would be gone. I was also conscious of the fact that that might mean my story in *Paradise* would soon be over as well.

Just as Osher was about to announce the first name, Jules interrupted. The whole thing sounded comically rehearsed. 'Sorry, Osher,' he said quietly, and Osher immediately paused.

I was amazed. But more than anything, I was impressed. I felt like Marti had just delivered on an unspoken contract.

Jules asked me for a moment outside, alone. 'You and I have a connection,' he said. 'Regardless of what I've done over the last few days, we could use *Paradise* to see if there is something actually there.'

I didn't really care much about what he was saying; for one thing, I didn't believe it. But I respected that Marti had pulled it off. She was making some bloody great TV.

Rose ceremonies on *Paradise* were one of the most interesting features of the show, one of the places contestants had the most autonomy. They were also an intersection of two different realities: the reality of the show and the reality of, well, reality. In the show, our relationship had clearly run its course. But in reality, I wanted to stay longer, be in more episodes and make more money. I didn't want the experience to end. And the relationship I'd established in the show was my only vehicle to manifest what I wanted in reality.

This was where Jules and I both found ourselves. We had a mutual goal: neither of us wanted this experience to end. I just happened to have slightly more feelings involved. We returned to the rose ceremony and, at the climax of the episode, Osher called my name. I stepped up to the pile of roses, performing the requisite solemn stare at the group of men. I waited a beat and then I said the name. 'Jules.'

The cameras packed up and I went back to my bure. I changed into a pair of the most horrendous long-john pyjama pants, which had absolutely no place in Fiji, and then headed back into the bar area, grabbing a cheese toastie on the way. I plonked myself down in a hammock by the pool and stared up at the stars.

I had been enjoying this so much, even through the most awful of emotions. It was so much better than *The Bachelor*, where I'd been practically invisible. But I prided myself on being authentic and what had just happened wasn't real. It was exactly what commenters on *Daily Mail* articles posited: that reality TV was fake, scripted; we were all acting. It was my most loathed criticism of the show because, for the most part, there was really nothing fake about it. But I knew that Jules hadn't stopped the rose ceremony because he liked me. He had stopped the rose ceremony because he had received a very compelling appeal from a charismatic producer five minutes beforehand. He had stopped the rose ceremony because he wanted to stay in Fiji.

Jules came over to find me in the hammock. I was halfway through the toastie, crumbs all over my chest. I told him I was upset, as he clambered into the hammock too. It really wasn't designed for two people. His feet were at my head and I tried to prop myself up on my elbows to speak to him properly.

'That's the first time we've been disingenuous,' I said to him.

He didn't disagree but he didn't have anything particularly insightful to add either. We looked at each other, pained. Our thoughts had been distorted by the events of the night, our differing perception of the situation and our exposed emotions. That night marked the beginning of an incredibly complex dance around what was real and what was not.

The next morning I woke up early, strangely energised. It was the same feeling you get after a break-up when you're momentarily motivated to start hitting the gym. The sleep hadn't helped; I still wanted to scream and cry and punch my pillow. But I also wanted to run. I wanted to try anything that would extract some of the painful emotion from my body. I grabbed the hot pink iPod nano tucked underneath my pillow.

I had keyed the camera lens in the top left corner and the shards of metal were rough under my fingertips. Recording devices were banned but I'd demonstrated to the minder who checked my bags for contraband that the camera no longer worked thanks to my engineering efforts.

I walked down a stretch of grass that separated our bures from the beach and jumped off a little embankment onto the soft sand. I scrolled through the iPod looking for the angriest song I could possibly find. It was a time capsule from my teenage years, which unfortunately for my present mood meant a lot more Ke$ha and less Rage Against The Machine. I scrolled until I found a song from My Chemical Romance and decided it would have to do.

With every footfall pounding into the beach, I told myself I wouldn't do it again. I repeated it, like a mantra. He'd told me he didn't like me, the rose ceremony had been a lie and I needed to move on. These were all facts I knew to be true. Today was a new day and I wouldn't allow myself to stay fixated on Jules. I'd fixate on literally anything else.

Thankfully, 'anything else' walked into *Paradise* just after lunchtime. He was known as 'Canadian Daniel'. He'd appeared on the first season of the Australian *Bachelor in Paradise*, and various versions of the US franchise. Daniel had made a name for himself on his first season of *Paradise*, with various macho declarations that he was going to 'steal' women from their established relationships. He'd called himself Geppetto because he was going to make the women in *Paradise* his puppets.

Though his reputation left much to be desired, when we spoke in person he seemed okay. He asked me questions about myself—rare both on TV shows and in real life—and seemed genuinely interested in what I had to say. Besides, it didn't really matter what Daniel had to say. In my mind, he was a means to an end. I wanted to show Jules that even though I'd given him a rose, I wasn't attached to him anymore. I was serious about moving on.

A couple of days earlier, on noticing how deflated I was, a producer had encouraged me to 'Kate Middleton about'. When Kate Middleton and Prince William had briefly split in 2007, she'd made sure she was seen absolutely everywhere. She'd gone out every single night and been photographed in all their favourite places. You couldn't open a copy of *The Sun* without seeing her in the social pages. The producer had encouraged me to do the same.

It was the TV version of posting thirst traps when a guy ghosts you. I was going to be everywhere, having so much fun, completely carefree. I think the same producer may have also steered Daniel in my direction, because when he received a date card it went to me. He was a nice guy and we had a fun day. We built a raft (this was still a reality TV show), traded some sexual innuendo and sipped on champagne before making out after I'd told him directly that I was looking for a rebound. Daniel gladly accepted the role.

We couldn't have been back from our date for more than ten minutes when Jules came to speak to me. Earlier that day, a couple of boys had given it to him straight: 'Alisha didn't keep you around so you could have a relationship with someone else.' Before they'd set him straight, I'm not sure he had realised that was the reality of the situation and now he was trapped by the expected rules of the game. There wasn't anything else for him to do in *Paradise*, no other story.

So now here he was, taking me on a date, leading me along the beachfront dotted with our bures and down into an area that I hadn't seen before. The camera crew was already set up. There were some cushions, the ubiquitous cheeseboard and the foundations of a fire. Jules motioned me over to the cushions and said he'd decided to set up the fire to 'reignite the spark'. I rolled my eyes and he gave me a half tickle, half squeeze, as he laughed.

Logically, I knew that Jules didn't have any creative control over the date, but my heart decided he'd requested a bonfire because of what I'd told him about bonfires with my family. Despite my mantras, and posturing with Daniel, this date was all that I had wanted. I wanted Jules to want me. And, more than anything, I wanted to kiss him again. Just once more. I told myself I didn't care whether it worked out in the end or not.

That night we had sex for the first time. For a moment, I just let myself forget. Forget about the TV production crew. Forget about the producers. Forget that there was a camera in the corner of our room filming. I didn't want to think too hard or too deeply.

If I did, I would start wondering about potential conversations he'd had with production while I was away on the date with Daniel. I'd think about a producer softly encouraging him to set something up. I'd think about Jules reading between the lines, considering whether he should just play into the narrative. Play into the only way for him to stay in *Paradise*. I didn't want to think about any of that. I really, really liked him.

I let myself fall into a different set of thoughts, a different reality. While there was technically a camera in the corner, there wasn't a crew filming. This wasn't a scene or a single date. It was midnight and we were alone. He was kissing me. He didn't have to be kissing me. He didn't have to be in my bed at all.

I thought back to our conversation about authenticity in the hammock. We could both feel the hand of production but neither of us had a solution. So here in his arms, with a thin white mosquito net framing our bodies, I decided that this was real. I decided that he had seen me go on the date and it had triggered some sort of emotion in him—some jealousy or clarity. I decided that he liked me and I let myself fall asleep with that thought.

CHAPTER 6

Umbrella of Ambiguity

Sleeping with Jules that night precipitated a cycle of desperate hope that I cringe to think back on now. During filming, when we returned home and as the show went to air, I unpicked every single interaction that I had with him, trying to find threads that affirmed that he liked me.

It wasn't all my fault. He did lead me on. But there were also moments, among the mixed messages, where he told me the truth and I chose to ignore it. The whole thing was painful.

For the rest of the show, Jules and I stayed in a strange holding pattern. We were 'together' but only because I let the physical element of our relationship sustain my hopes of a happy ending and I'm not sure he knew what else to do.

Jules and I received a date card in the last days of filming. It was a little push from production to frame us as one of the four couples whose relationship would become the focus of the show's finale episodes. It was a few days after the bonfire and we travelled twenty minutes to a beach where we were greeted by a table and chairs sat partially submerged in the water. The table was set with kitsch crockery, little cupcakes and stacks of macarons. Producers had cleverly labelled the date 'a high tea in the sea'. Before we sat down at the table, we did multiple takes walking down the beach with a drone following overhead. Each time, as our feet touched the cool Fijian water, Jules offered me a piggyback to my chair. We shot this four times and at no point did it get more graceful.

The date started like most of ours did: exchanging one-liners, flirty banter and leaning into whatever activity had been prepared for us. Once we were seated, Jules tried his first-ever macaron and I prepared to cut a small cake in the middle of the table.

As I reached for the knife, Jules raised that classic birthday party tradition. 'What's the thing? If the knife comes out . . .' he started.

'If the knife comes out dirty, you have to kiss the nearest boy,' I finished, jamming the knife into the cake to ensure it came out very dirty.

Jules told me to behave myself and then held my face in both his hands and kissed me. I could've just left the date there and not pushed any further. The drones took shots of us floating in the water on our backs among the coral reef, and the camera operator got some cutaways of us making out against the idyllic tropical backdrop. It would be a nice feel-good filler date for the end of the season. And that's what production wanted, but I just couldn't leave it there.

'What do you think of Alisha and Jules?' I asked him.

'I think it's weird,' he replied.

'They're bloody weird characters, Alisha and Jules. No one else understands them. I don't think they even understand themselves, but they're at a level where they like that ambiguity.'

'I feel like moving forward under an umbrella of ambiguity might be best for us,' Jules told me.

I couldn't quite believe the pattern of words that had come out of his mouth. We were right back to him electing not to emotionally pursue me, only this time, he'd managed to be even more creative with his language. He'd just held my face in his hands and kissed me and now he was sitting here telling me our relationship should move forward under an 'umbrella of ambiguity'. That wasn't a thing, nobody said that.

When the date wrapped, the producer allocated to Jules directed him over to a camera set up further down the beach.

I stayed, sitting alone in the middle of the sea, contemplating his weasel words. In my post-date interview with my producer, Laura, I broke down. He was telling me the truth. He wasn't into me. And he definitely didn't want to be in a relationship with me. Yet here I was, shooting these scenes, falling deeper and deeper in love with him as he slowly rejected me.

I became frustrated. 'What the fuck am I still doing here?' I snapped at Laura. I couldn't see how the story was going to end, because I was blind to the fact that Jules conclusively rejecting me for a second time after another four-episode build-up was a perfectly satisfying climax in the eyes of production. Laura placated me. She was doing her job, which was to keep propelling me towards the final rituals of *Bachelor in Paradise*—meeting each other's friends and family and the commitment ceremony. There was less payoff for the audience if I was to just walk away without explanation after our high tea in the sea. The producers wanted conflict. They wanted charged emotions. But preferably they would bubble away before erupting at the grand finale.

Jules and I had talked about the meeting each other's friends and family part quite a bit while in our holding pattern. It was fraught. While his feelings for me were still under an 'umbrella of ambiguity', as he had so poetically described, neither of us could resist the novelty of flying our two best friends all the way to Fiji on Warner Brothers' dollar. We had talked about

Hannah and Jimmy all season and couldn't quite believe that we had an opportunity to involve them in an experience that we both had so much fun with, despite our recent turmoil.

The friends and family meeting was production's ultimate mechanism to whittle down the final four couples. While Jules and I had a perfunctory conversation on camera agreeing to proceed to the next stage, other couples came to different conclusions. Generally, at the behest of the producers. There were Alex and Caroline, who were both from America. They had a short conversation agreeing to continue their relationship back in the United States—and meet their family and friends over there rather than have Warner Brothers pay for it. Another couple, Zoe and Mack, had only shared a kiss just the night before. Mack seemed keen to keep the party going, but Zoe saw her out. She told Mack it was far too soon for them to be meeting friends, let alone family, and wrapped up their relationship in an efficient, ten-minute chat.

Once half the cast had left for the airport, the remaining couples were split up and sequestered. We were driven back to the Naviti and put into shared rooms. My roommate was Tenille. We bonded over the chaos of the last few weeks and smoked an entire packet of her Winnie Blues in less than two hours, lamenting the 'situationships' we had found ourselves in with each drag.

Tenille had been through the wringer too. What she'd started to explore with Ivan became far too intense, far too quickly. Ivan had been devastated by the development and a casualty of his heartache was my pink iPod nano, which he'd taken out on a paddleboard and subsequently dropped in the water. I was pissed. Tenille had since partnered up with Nathan Favro. He was a kind-enough guy and very good-looking, but Tenille felt he was only emotionally open towards her when the cameras were rolling. She didn't trust that he genuinely liked her. She thought he was performing and was worried that he'd drop her as soon as they left the structured confines of the show.

Our minder during this sequester was a producer called Tess. Tess was cool. She happily went to a nearby convenience store to procure us another packet of cigarettes and let us have more than one glass of wine with our room service, flouting production's general rule. This kindness seemed practically saintly to two women locked in a small hotel room.

As we worked our way through a bottle of wine, Tess effortlessly joined the bitchfest about our respective men. Tenille and I had just been discussing how strange and special it was to get to know someone without seeing their social media—how they brand themselves to the world—and Tess chimed in with the offer to let us stalk Jules' and Nathan's Instagram profiles.

It was a massive no-no from a producer, an absolute wind-fall for us.

We started with Nathan. He was every bit the influencer. All his pictures were sharp and effortlessly cool. His grid was consistently filtered with desaturated blues and deep, golden tans. A festival here, a house party there. We commented on how perfect his life looked. I think Tenille was a little taken aback by just how considered it was.

Jules was next. It was very Jules. Very indie, lots of craft beer. Lots of his best friend's band. I opened one of the thumbnails and could see Jimmy tagged; with just another click I could explore a whole person's life. I felt so powerful flicking through the app's windows. I kept scrolling. A series of photos of Jules in hospital, when he'd broken his leg—my fingers prickled as I remembered him touching them to his shin. In February 2018 came a bunch of snow shots. The location tag said he'd been in Japan. One picture had a cute, blonde girl in frame.

I clicked through to her profile and discovered a whole new collection of images. On 6 November, the day before I'd flown to Fiji, she'd uploaded a picture of her and Jules leaning against a fence on a coastal walk, two red hearts in the caption.

I scrolled down. A picture of them in the snow. A picture of them exploring the streets of Tokyo. I turned the laptop slightly towards the girls. They'd been observing over my shoulder as I explored.

'Fuck,' I said.

'Fuck,' they replied.

I attempted to rationalise it. Maybe she was a cousin? Maybe just a really good friend?

Tess wasn't as forgiving. 'What a dog,' she scoffed and stood up to order another bottle of wine.

I got up from the bed and slid open the balcony door. I think Jules had told me about this girl. When he said he'd never had a girlfriend, I pressed and asked if he'd ever had anything 'like one'. Someone he had feelings for, someone he'd spent a lot of time with. He'd mentioned a name, and the name that he mentioned matched the name I'd seen on the screen. My mind continued to explain the image away. I was doing the same thing I'd been doing the entire time: telling myself a different story. A story that suited me better.

I sat in a wicker chair in the corner of the balcony, now scrolling through Tenille's iPod, trying to find the perfect soundtrack to my sadness. I closed my eyes and let the ridiculous techno beat of 'Now You're Gone' by Basshunter envelop my body. I'd also 'borrowed' Tenille's pack of cigarettes and inhaled as deeply as an asthmatic who didn't really know how to smoke could. In truth, I looked pretty unhinged, chain-smoking and bopping along to the Eurodance beats. It was as if I had tried to match the absurdity of the scene to the intensity of my emotions. I kept telling myself that tomorrow morning I'd get to see Hannah, and Hannah would know what to do.

Hannah did know what to do, but she was careful with my feelings as she expressed herself as diplomatically as she could. She could tell that I liked him. I talked a mile a minute at her, describing every little ebb and flow of his affection throughout the show. Despite what I'd seen the night before and my ever-increasing doubt, I fell straight back into waxing lyrical about how incredible Jules was and how I'd never met anyone like him.

'You're going to love him,' I told her.

Hannah did not love him. In their chat, he described our relationship as a 'unique friendship' and, free of my infatuation, Hannah could see that he didn't see a future for us at all. She told the producers as much, making it clear he was basically saying that we were friends with benefits. With me, though, she was gentler, leaving space for me to make my own decision.

Jimmy was more direct. As I related our experience—with appropriate emphasis and dramatic pauses bookending when Jules chose not to 'emotionally pursue' me and said we should leave *Paradise* under an 'umbrella of ambiguity'—his face told me that this was not the first time he had heard a creative turn of phrase from his friend. He advised me to grill him for the clarity I'd been searching for. No umbrellas, no ambiguity. He told me I needed to get a yes or no answer.

There was one last stop before the commitment ceremony: the ritualistic final date where Jules and I would compare notes about what our friends thought and how we were feeling, before choosing whether or not to spend the last night before the grand finale together. Production was desperate for us to make it to the commitment ceremony, but my patience was fast running out.

Speaking to Jimmy and Hannah had brought our relationship from the show world to the real world. It started to draw me out of my denial. I didn't want another placeholder date taking me closer to what I increasingly felt was going to be a conclusive rejection. I didn't want to put on a gorgeous dress and face full of make-up only for Jules to call me his friend.

When a producer realised I wasn't going to float on to the finale, Marti was sent to see me. But this time, I was implacable.

I told her I was going to give Jules an ultimatum. If he couldn't tell me that we were anything more than friends, I would leave tonight. On my own terms.

Under masses of fairy lights and over a final cheeseboard, I laid out my position. Jules wanted to continue on to the commitment ceremony and clearly hadn't expected this hard conversation. He proposed that we just put emotions aside and enjoy our remaining time in Fiji. Just one last night. But there had already been too many 'one last nights' so I persisted with an incredibly uncomfortable-looking Jules, who finally shared his feelings after yet another protracted pause.

'You said to me, sort of halfway through this, that you want the bloke who looks at you when you walk into the room and he knows one hundred per cent that he made the right decision. He thinks, that's my Alisha. In that moment, I felt that I couldn't give that to you, so I thought to myself, this girl deserves more than me.'

Even then, in Jules' final speech, I still thought his answer might change. I thought 'in that moment' meant he now felt differently in this moment.

But he continued. 'At this stage right now, I feel like I can't give you what you deserve.'

My mind raced, registering his words despite my perpetual hope.

'I know that I can't give you one hundred per cent, I can't give you full commitment.'

As the conversation started to circle, I asked him what message he thought he had been sending me. When I brought up the fact we'd slept together, he told me he'd been trying to be friendly—he was just trying to enjoy my company.

With that, I couldn't take him seriously anymore. I had my answer and this time I decided to listen. I gave him a hug. He kissed my head and then I left, walking away as I had planned, finally following through on the boundaries that I'd set for myself.

I walked out of the date and straight into an interview, exhausted and ready to tie it all up. His idea that sleeping with somebody was just being friendly had at least provided some levity, and I managed to relax. But right until the very end, our ridiculous dance continued. Just as I was joking with the producer that I might have to hit up Canadian Daniel again—asking, 'When's the next flight to Vancouver?'—Jules interrupted my interview. He said he didn't understand the ultimatum. He asked if I'd be happy to see him again.

'No!' I responded indignantly. 'I'm electing to not emotion-ally pursue you, Jules.'

My girl-power moment finally came. After another hug Jules walked away, asking producers if he could take his microphone off. There was no more story to tell.

I was picked up from the Naviti the next morning at five a.m. A three-hour drive to the airport alone with your own thoughts is just what everyone wants after being rejected on a reality TV show that will be broadcast to half a million people.

One of my favourite minders took pity on me and gave me my phone for the ride, against protocol. We weren't supposed to get our phones back until we landed in Sydney, for fear we would pre-arrange pap shots of our airport arrival. I guess the minder thought my puffy face and general sad vibe weren't really camera-ready.

I couldn't have contacted anyone anyway, because I hadn't paid my phone bill. I couldn't go on Facebook or check Instagram, so I just listened to the U2 album that was forcefully loaded on everyone's phones years ago. Needless to say, I was feeling very sorry for myself. When I landed in Sydney and hastily got my phone sorted, the dread of what would happen next started to take over.

The first thing I did was check the forums. They'd been discussing the series most days before I'd left to film and I picked up where I had left off. I wanted to know what they knew, what they didn't and what they thought. They had pictures of Cat and I arriving in Fiji, pushing our trolleys through the airport. They had pictures of Richie and us playing football in the early days of shooting. And they speculated as to when we were eliminated, relishing the fact that Cat, the mean girl, looked like an early out because she was back on social media.

I skimmed faster, looking for Bobette's name. About halfway through filming, she'd posted an article announcing that Jules and a girl called Shannon Baff from my original *Bachelor* season would both be on the show. Shannon had been on the show and she'd partnered up with an American guy called Connor in Fiji, although no one had really understood the match and the cast had speculated they'd pre-gamed because they stuck together like glue through the month of filming. Bobette, however, predicted that Shannon was going to end up with Jules, and fawned over their supposed perfect match. I felt a strange rush of jealousy, even though I was well aware of what had actually happened.

The second thing I did was reach out to Jules. I had lied: I was happy to see him again. In fact, seeing him was all I could think about. I found him on Instagram and messaged him after sitting on the idea for all of half an hour. Terrible willpower. I couldn't commit to my declaration. I needed to know what he thought of the wild four weeks of shooting we'd just been through. I needed to know what he thought of me.

I thought that maybe without cameras and microphones, the pressure would be off and something would be different. I thought he might watch our first date when it aired, see our chemistry through the screen and think, *Fuck, I've really fucked this up.* I sat on my couch, looking at my own blue bubble, waiting for his reply. He messaged back an hour later saying he'd been nervous about who was going to message first. Below that sat his number.

We quickly fell back into our old pattern. Jules would offer me breadcrumbs, giving just enough time, energy and affection to make me think that he might like me. We'd message constantly throughout the day and I'd search his texts for clues. He would call me beautiful in a wall of text and I would fixate on that word alone.

The messages made me obsess over seeing him again. I was desperate to see how we would interact with each other in the real world, but he didn't seem that interested in making it happen. And whenever I decided to create some distance, he'd somehow reel me back in.

The first time I really tried to create some space was after a handful of weeks where he'd ducked any plans to meet up in person. I'd woken up to a good morning message from him. He'd sent a link to the song 'Something About Us' by Daft Punk and the words *'Give it a listen'* in all caps. I clicked on the link, half asleep, and the sound carried through the room from my iPhone speaker. I loved Daft Punk, but I didn't know this song. It started with soft piano and the sound of falling rain, before introducing a funky, very Daft Punk, beat. When some synthesised vocals cut in just after the one-minute mark I was suddenly very awake.

The lyrics were unbelievably romantic. I could feel myself getting agitated. It was the absolute peak of his head-fuckery, a blatant crumb. Or was it? Was I reading too much into it? The last verse of the song played as I spiralled.

Fuck this guy, seriously. Did he mean for me to overanalyse this? Or was he just trying to send me a song that he liked and I was being a freak? Whatever his intentions, I could feel my whole self-worth back under his thumb. It was too much; I felt like I was going to pop.

I rang the show psych on the way to work. Alex encouraged me to take a break from contacting him, to recalibrate myself. I took her advice.

Jules was the culmination of every mistake I'd ever made looking for love. I was twisting myself into whatever version of whatever person I thought he would like the most. I'd laugh at bad jokes, pretend I was fine when I was angry and play the cool girl lest he think I was clingy or desperate.

It was like I was sixteen again. Back then, I'd been so desperate for this older guy to like me that I did anything to impress him. I remember him inviting me to a house party. I was still in high school, and everyone else there were first-year uni students. Just like with Jules, I wanted them all to think I was cool and casual, that I was up for anything. The illusion didn't last long when, sitting in a musty-smelling bedroom, one of his friends passed me the bong they were all smoking.

I looked down at it, the wisdom of Healthy Harold still very fresh in my mind, but wanting them all—wanting him—to like me. The allure of his approval was too intoxicating and I decided that I would do it.

A moment later, he stopped me. 'Are you joking?'

I'd put my mouth on the cone piece, the hole you pack the weed into. I didn't know what I was doing, I'd just wanted him to think I'd fit into his world. I was mortified.

It wasn't the first time, and it wouldn't be the last, that I'd do anything to impress a man. Sometimes it was pretending I was obsessed with Sum 41 when I was briefly seeing a drummer in a pop punk band, other times it was telling someone I wrote 'prose' in my free time, because I knew they were majoring in English literature.

Again, I was back to believing that physical connection was a precursor to a relationship. I thought that if Jules made out with me, or slept with me, it must mean he was in love with me. I'd done this with Joe, my big love at uni. Joe had been cheating on me all throughout our relationship and eventually some friends of mine found out and decided to tell me. They told me that Joe had been having 'three a.m. Netflix nights' with a girl in the law faculty. It was someone he'd told me was just a friend, that I had nothing to worry about. I wasn't stupid, I knew what three a.m. Netflix nights meant.

I broke up with Joe the same afternoon and drove myself home, pulling my shitbox Corolla over halfway to sob violently when '3AM' by Matchbox Twenty played on the radio.

Joe started dating the law student and I thought that I'd never recover. But weeks later, when I learnt that we were both set to attend the Australian Young Labor Conference in Canberra, I put plan 'Win Joe back' into action. I decided I'd seduce him at the Student Unity Faction Dinner at Dickson Asian Noodle House and packed my most enticing outfit: a red bandage dress, a statement necklace and laser-cut suede heels, a staple of 2014.

It didn't take much to get Joe back to the hostel we were all staying at. We slept together and I thought I'd won. If he'd slept with me, it must mean there was something he couldn't deny between us. We'd be back on track.

But in the morning, it was apparent that nothing had changed. We carpooled back to Sydney with our comrades after the conference. He didn't speak a word to me and my self-assurance quickly turned to shame. I later learnt that Joe told his new girlfriend exactly what had happened. He really liked her and wanted it to work. It took me years to learn my lesson and I hurt a whole string of people until I did. I had just felt like it was the only way to have him recognise me. It was my only power.

And now I was doing it again. I had placed the power of determining my value in somebody else's hands. I was consumed by Jules and I resented how much he dictated my emotions. He'd affected me so strongly that the people around me could feel how deflated I was. Mum said she'd never seen me with such a heavy heart. My break from him lasted all of a fortnight. He rang me just before Christmas and I caved. I was back on the roller-coaster again.

It wasn't until the show started airing that my focus shifted for the first time in a long time from whether Jules liked me to whether Australia liked me. I felt quietly confident leaving *Paradise* that people would receive a deeper understanding of who I was as a person, even if that was through the frame of my tumultuous relationship with Jules. Though I would have to wade through my previously established reputation as a sheep and mean girl before getting any reprieve.

My post-episode routine of consuming every single piece of commentary I could find returned in full force. On the night I entered *Paradise*, Bobette reacted, 'Alicia. Meh.' And following my first kiss with Paddy: 'Paddy and Alicia, realising they're low-tier contestants, combine their E-grade assets with the hope of scraping into level D.'

I couldn't help but laugh; Bobette really had a way with words, even if she neglected to spell my name right. The reception was similar across every single platform and I had to grin and bear it until the fourth episode of the season went to air. The episode where Jules would enter.

Jules came up to Sydney so we could watch the episode together. It was one of the few times over the course of the last four months I had willed him to come and see me and he had actually shown up. We sat on the floor of my living room, watching the scenes of us feeding each other asparagus and chocolate-dipped strawberries go to air. I was living one of the moments I'd been waiting for, one of the moments I thought something between us would shift. In the months since filming, I considered that maybe I had gaslit myself. That maybe I'd built up that first date in *Paradise* to be something that it wasn't. But watching it back, months later, it was clear it was a good date. Australia thought so too. The comments under a Facebook clip of the scene were some of the nicest I'd ever seen. 'Oh I just love this . . . super cute,' and 'They'll make it to the end.' In my fantasy, Jules, watching the scene and seeing the public's response, would finally trigger him to register our chemistry and we'd make out the rest of the night. Instead, we got drunk and he ordered McDonald's on UberEats. I ate two McChickens while listening to Jules snore, passed out in my bed.

The public's approval was a welcome consolation as the episodes continued and I relived all the worst parts of the show.

What I quickly discovered is that in watching yourself on TV, you experience the emotions even more deeply than when they were happening the first time. This time the memories of Jules ditching me for Tenille and ignoring me for days were accompanied by a sombre soundtrack, amplifying the feelings of rejection and humiliation. This time there was an editor shaping the story to elicit an emotional response—it was no longer two humans muddling their way through, thinking they were in control of their narrative.

When the episode featuring the rose ceremony that Jules interrupted went to air, I messaged Hannah, remembering that she hadn't actually seen it play out. I had tried to paint it for her in big descriptive brushstrokes over the past four months but despite my best representations, she hadn't felt my emotions until she saw them. Post-production made sure they included the most painful and raw of my reactions. Like me sitting in a yellow tartan dress in the interview chair explaining that I didn't feel confident through my first season of *The Bachelor*. That I had been full of self-doubt. 'I came into *Paradise*, and I made myself be confident,' I told the producer. 'I made myself know my self-worth and in this moment Jules took it all away.' On screen, I was red-faced and fighting back tears. As I sat watching it back on the couch, I was red-faced and messaging Hannah wildly.

'Dude, people are going to be so disappointed in me lol,' I said, in anticipation of my capitulation.

'No, they will understand,' Hannah comforted me. *'Every girl has been there.'*

This was bad, but I knew it got worse. Watching it play back on screen brought back all the hurt I had felt in the moment, and this time with anger as well.

Hannah was angry too. *'I want you to cut him off. Don't talk to him anymore.'*

'I won't. He's done,' I replied.

And for once I kept my word. By the time the final episode aired Jules and I had stopped talking. Watching the continued scenes of me being messed around by his mixed messages provided me with some sense of objectivity about how badly he had treated me. And people were really shitty at him. Shittier than I expected. Articles detailed his deceptions, podcasts lambasted his behaviour towards me and it all felt incredibly validating. It was as if I trusted the audience's reaction more than my own.

The whole thing was almost all over. I was finally going to be free after six months of the most frustrating cycle of wishing and wanting, most of it that I'd brought on myself. All that was left was to record a reunion episode—our contracts compelled us to be involved.

The reunion was shot on a colourful set in the basement of the Channel Ten building in Pyrmont. I was excited to do it. I was buoyed by the response to the season. Even the forums had come around to me. When Jules first rejected me for Tenille, Bobette had commented that they couldn't quite believe it, but they were feeling sympathy for me. And a couple of episodes later, Bobette even suggested they might be warming up to me. The feeling was addictive, and I wanted to keep the momentum going. I had a feeling about what I needed to do in the eyes of the audience. This season Jules was the bad person and I was good. He had hurt me; he was the manipulator and he needed to be held accountable. When Jules and I were called to sit with Osher, to reflect on our journey and reveal what had happened when the cameras stopped rolling, I went to town. I really laid into him, listing a whole range of different things that had happened over the months since filming that had fucked with my head. I even used the opportunity to return some underwear he'd left at my house. That didn't make the final cut.

It was the ending everyone expected. But when we wrapped for the night, I didn't feel happy, I didn't feel empowered. I felt kind of mean. I felt like I'd been led by the narrative that had been built around us. I didn't know whether pouring oil on the fire was really what he deserved. To this day, I can't quite decide.

When the reunion went to air, I didn't watch it with anybody. I watched it at home, alone, letting it wash over me. I cringed watching myself act so aggressively towards Jules. The person on screen wasn't a version of myself that I was proud of, even though everyone online seemed to be cheering for me. I went to bed as soon as the episode finished, not even stopping to watch *Bachelor Unpacked*.

It would've been nearing three a.m. when I was woken by the harsh ringing of our old-school brass doorbell. It was the type you twist to ring and the person behind the door was really going for it. I moved through the dark, bleary-eyed, and was greeted by an UberEats driver pushing a brown paper bag into my hand.

'Jules!' he said loudly, leaving me in the doorway and walking back to his beat-up Toyota Corolla.

Half-awake, I looked down at the brown paper bag, now in my hand. *Jules? What?* I walked back inside and made myself comfortable on our lumpy couch, ripping open the bag. It contained a kebab in classic packaging with 'Tasty' emblazoned in a red-and-yellow eighties-style font. Next to that, in black pen, was 'Jules'.

Sorry, what? A kebab with Jules' name on it. What could it possibly mean? I came up with two theories.

Jules had sent it himself. It was an olive branch. The last few weeks had been rough, the reunion had been rough. He was reaching out in the only way he felt he could. I liked this theory; it meant we'd be okay after all this. He must have been having some late-night feels about the whole thing being over.

My other theory was that it was from someone who had watched the show. They felt bad for me. It was a comfort kebab. I don't know how they would've gotten my address, but maybe it was someone close to me, a friend.

I ruminated about the potential mystery sender of the kebab late into the next afternoon, when I decided to share it on Instagram. I grabbed a picture from my camera roll I'd taken the night before.

'Okay, who sent me a kebab at 2.30 a.m. under the name Jules?' I wrote.

I wasn't game to send him a text about it directly; we were at the stage of sending coded messages through public social media posts. I thought maybe the Instagram story would flush out who had sent it, even if I risked being disappointed it wasn't Jules.

Later that night, I regaled a group of friends with the story at a birthday party at a local pub. I showed them what I'd uploaded to Instagram. Before I could launch any deeper into my theories, my friend Evan piped up. He'd done this exact thing before. I asked him what he meant. He had sent a late-night kebab to someone he cared about?

Evan shook his head. He'd ordered something on UberEats while drunk and it had been delivered to the house of the girl he'd been casually seeing. My jaw dropped open. I was such an idiot. Jules had been trying to order *himself* a kebab. His kebab had ended up at my house because three weeks earlier, he'd ordered drunk McDonald's to my address as we'd watched our first date air over bottles of wine. Evan had explained away my complex mystery so quickly. The reality was quite simple: a boy had been trying to order himself a drunk kebab. I felt bad. I bet he had been really disappointed when it didn't come.

That kebab was emblematic of the way I approached everything with Jules: the constant search for clues that he felt the same way as I felt about him. I had constructed a complicated story, with motives and emotions, that couldn't have been further from the truth. I'd done it from the very beginning, from our very first date. I'd gone back to my bure, put my head down to sleep and constructed a version of who I thought he was, extrapolated from the tiny bits I'd actually seen. I'd fallen for that version, for what he represented to me. He had been going to be my redemption—to give me an identity after I'd left *The Bachelor* feeling like nothing. He was going to be my love story.

In all of this, I'd never actually given him a chance to show me who he really was at all. It was funny, because the way that Jules had initially approached Tenille was in fact exactly how I had approached him.

There's a word for what I felt for Jules. It's called limerence, a special brand of infatuation. It's sustained when there is a certain balance of hope and uncertainty. The basis for limerent love is not in objective reality but in reality as it is perceived. I'd just reshaped a chicken kebab into a grand romantic gesture. The ridiculousness of it all might have been just the thing to finally shake me out of it.

CHAPTER 7

Back to Reality

The backlash against Jules only grew in severity in the days following the finale. What had started as pretty standard post-show stuff devolved into some of the most vile abuse I'd ever witnessed off the back of a TV show. I didn't think the viewer response could get worse than what Cat, Romy and I had experienced, but somehow strangers on the internet managed.

Comments calling Jules a dick were soon replaced by people calling him a cunt. Comments labelling him selfish turned into strings of snake emojis, posted incessantly. Commenters became more and more extreme, emboldened by one another, joining the pile-on and tagging their friends to come enjoy the onslaught.

Two themes became popular.

'Seriously, when are you coming out, mate?'

'ASD???'

Jules couldn't have simply not been that into me: he was either gay or he was on the spectrum. The pack grasped their words as weapons, choosing the labels they thought would hurt the most. In their ignorant eyes, I guess they believed those were the worst things a person could be.

I had just been flicking through a fresh round of comments when a shrill ring interrupted me. It was Mum. We were clearly filling our time in the same way and she was practically in tears when I answered. She told me that she had been reading the comments about Jules and that it wasn't okay. My mother is a woman who feels everything deeply. She rages at injustice and cries at the sombre subplot of a kid's movie. She absorbs people's emotions like a sponge.

She asked me to do something. To fix it. Her appeal quickly shook me out of any lingering schadenfreude.

When I hung up, I opened my camera roll. I found a picture of Jules and me in happier times in Byron Bay, two months after the show. We were on a beach; I was in a rust-coloured bikini, giving him a piggyback. We posed with sunnies on, our hands cheekily framing our faces.

I typed out a caption, trying to find balance. I didn't want to be a doormat but I felt it was time to let sleeping dogs lie. I said that I was heartened that people had gotten to see a fuller picture of my personality through *Paradise* and that I was appreciating the love, but I could still vividly remember how it felt to be targeted on social media and now my heart was hurting for Jules.

My heart did genuinely hurt for Jules. The response wasn't proportionate to the crime. I ended by saying it was time to bury the hatchet and get back to normal programming: electing Labor governments and trying to get better at make-up. I ended the post with a peace sign and the little smiling emoji framed by hearts. I felt a weight lift as soon as I hit upload.

The flood of responses on my page could not have been in starker contrast to those on Jules': where there had once been streams of comments eviscerating my character, there were now hundreds of people telling me how proud they were of me. Words like wonderful, strong and kind had replaced evil, nasty and sheep. People called me pretty and no one commented on my nose. Some comments called for me to be the Bachelorette, others (generously) prime minister. It was everything I'd wanted since pressing submit on that original *Bachelor* application form. It was validation. It was affirmation. It was confirmation that people liked me.

I even finally received an invite to something. It might have been an invitation to *Maxim Australia*'s eighth birthday party at a questionable bar in Kings Cross—but it was something.

That was why I was all the more confused when I felt so empty.

This was what I had wanted, wasn't it?

I'd wanted positive comments. I'd wanted Bobette to like me. And I'd wanted to be invited to things. But all I felt was empty. It seemed like a trick: the tide of public opinion had started to flow in my favour but it was simply momentum, not anything meaningful. I had come to see how fickle we could be.

In the weeks following the finale, whenever anybody raved at me about the amazing reception or how well I did on the show, I would maniacally scroll back through a year of Instagram photos and show them my 'elimination' photo from the first season of *The Bachelor* and the comments below it. I'd point out the people tagging their friends. I'd point out the comments labelling me a bad person.

Now I was good, but only because someone else was worse.

With the show finally over, I was left with the ashes of a romantic obsession, a group of colleagues that didn't exactly know what to make of my two starkly different lives and a self-esteem that had been comprehensively destroyed. I couldn't open Instagram without comparing who I was, what I looked like and where I was going with whoever popped up first on the screen. On paper, everything looked great. But when I finally got the adulation I'd been hoping for, it didn't seem to be the silver bullet to happiness that I thought it would be. Instead, old insecurities were replaced by new. Why do my photos not look like her photos? Why have they received that opportunity and I haven't?

I remember visiting some *Bachelor in Paradise* castmates in Melbourne not long after the show and asking one of the girls to edit a photo that we'd taken on a night out. I wanted the look, I wanted that Instagram face—smooth, flawless, plump and tan. She commandeered my phone for a full five minutes, and when she gave it back I couldn't have been happier with the results. She'd etched away everything I didn't like about myself. Looking back at it now, my first instinct is to laugh, to prevent myself being captured by how depressing it is. I look like a carrot. I have half a shoulder and a completely different nose. I don't know who the person in the photo is. I think I feel sorry for her, but I know she's just trying her best.

I poured myself into work as a sort of salve to the superficial, thinking that the virtue in electing progressive governments would temper my existential crisis. The entire team at NSW

Labor worked nonstop throughout 2019. There was a state election in March and a federal election in May. During the first few months of the year, we arranged countless rallies and launches in the hopes of electing the opposition leaders Michael Daley and Bill Shorten. It was punishing work but a campaign environment is like no other so we were all happy to be there. Kaila led the team through it all, just as optimistic as always. We held fundraising dinners declaring the state to be 'Fortress NSW' and organised buses plastered with 'Schools and Hospitals before Stadiums' to drive around the suburbs of Western Sydney.

We kept the mood up through both elections, declaring Michael Daley the future premier of New South Wales and Bill Shorten the future prime minister of Australia in Instagram posts and Facebook statuses, as though if we typed out the letters often enough we would will them into existence.

Neither were elected.

The office felt defeated. Months and months of hard work, of getting up before the sun and getting to bed far too late, seemingly for nothing.

Then ICAC came along in August.

ICAC was the Independent Commission Against Corruption in New South Wales, an agency responsible for investigating corrupt conduct in public administration, particularly in politics. It had claimed some massive scalps, such as former NSW premier Barry O'Farrell, who had 'forgotten' receiving a 3000-dollar bottle of Penfolds Grange from private company Australian Water Holdings. In August, ICAC was knocking on the Labor Party's door. A series of public hearings began related to an investigation that centred around whether officers of the Labor Party, party members and political donors had carried out a scheme to circumvent electoral laws. The allegation was that a Chinese billionaire had donated 100,000 dollars to the Party in an Aldi bag (a colourful detail that captured lots of media attention). The lawful limit for a donation from an individual was 5000 dollars. The donation had been concealed through a stack of false declarations, made by people who were found not to be in the Labor Party, or even to know what the Labor Party was. They'd been asked to sign a piece of paper by someone they respected, so they did what they were told.

Since the beginning of hearings, the office had been eerie. Each day we'd come to work, refresh the ICAC website and be greeted with a new set of exhibits that included references to colleagues that we'd worked with for years. Little was communicated to the current staff about what was happening or what to expect; everything was just tense, as we watched it all play out in the newspapers and on the nightly news.

On the third day of hearings, Kaila was called to give evidence. She testified that she knew about the donation and hadn't disclosed it to the relevant authorities. She struggled to hold back tears while she explained that she'd helped keep the donations quiet because she'd been scared for the office and scared for the reputation of the Labor Party.

By that afternoon, she'd been suspended as general secretary. Two months later, she resigned.

The Party and the media buzzed with gossip throughout it all, with everyone ready and waiting to throw their two cents in. Some unnamed insiders said her resignation should've come sooner, before ICAC even happened, others attributed her undoing to the toxic culture she'd been marinating in.

The Party's parliamentary leader, Jodi McKay, who wouldn't have been installed without Kaila, called her a 'broken person', who would never work for the Labor Party again. It seemed like everyone had a soundbite, an opinion and a hot take. But for me, Kaila was a friend, a mentor and most importantly a human being. Someone who had made a mistake. In politics, it is often said, 'Live by the sword, die by the sword' but to see it twisted in, with such pleasure and in such close proximity, was incredibly difficult to witness.

A few weeks after she resigned, I visited Kaila to check in. I leant against her kitchen island as she made us two cups of tea. Despite everything that had happened in past months—the cameras and microphones thrust into her face, her life and career treated as delicious gossip—she still smiled and joked.

We spoke about what she might do next, with her whole life ahead of her at thirty-three. 'Maybe *Survivor*?' I laughed. She'd become accustomed to backstabbing, but we weren't sure how she'd go with the fire-making.

When I was halfway through the cup of lemongrass and ginger tea she'd made, Kaila dragged a garbage bag full of corporate clothing into the living room. She told me she didn't have use for them anymore. She pulled an assortment of power suits, midi dresses and blazers out onto the rug and went through each item, pausing to hold some up and tell me when she'd bought it.

A knee-length cobalt blue dress from Cue for the faction meeting that would elect her. A coral-coloured Scanlan Theodore blazer for her first trip to Canberra as general secretary. A khaki jacket from Decjuba with gold buttons on the wrists that she'd grabbed from World Square before a particularly heated internal committee meeting. She pushed them all towards me. 'Take whatever!' she said with an exasperated smile. It was just so Kaila. At the end of the day, regardless of whatever her detractors wanted to level at her, it had rarely been about her at all. It had always been about others. Always about the Party.

I obligingly gathered a few things and we said goodbye. I hugged her tight, with the bundle of clothes pressed between us, hoping she could feel how much I cared through osmosis. I wore the coral-coloured blazer into work the next day. A little piece of Kaila, defiantly walking back into Sussex Street.

My love life was going just as well as work. Trying to escape my hangover from Jules, I updated my profile on all the dating apps. Hannah and I had just moved into a new and improved home in Summer Hill. We had left the mismatched second-hand couches from our youth behind, signing a year-long lease on a small two-bedroom unit, with stainless steel appliances and a white laminate kitchen. It was everything I'd ever wanted. No dowdy cabinets from the seventies and for the first time in my life we even had a dishwasher.

I'd joked to Hannah as we searched for a place that the deciding factor was going to be whether I felt proud to bring a boy back. And at Summer Hill I felt so proud. It was my bachelorette pad. I made myself comfortable on our new grey lounge set and navigated between Tinder, Bumble and Hinge.

Tinder was the biggest pain to sift through, filled with guys holding dead fish trophies and bios claiming they were six foot tall 'because apparently that matters'. But I had a theory that Tinder could also bring the biggest reward: well-adjusted men in their thirties who had been in long-term relationships that hadn't worked out due to timing. These hypothetical men would be on Tinder because it would be the only online dating app they'd heard of. I thought my theory had legs so I kept the app in the mix, swiping through endless profiles.

Dotted in the hellscape I found a handful of quality candidates and padded out my roster with a couple of people from my Instagram DMs, and an ex-boyfriend for good measure.

I started with David. He was a political reporter who used his work headshot on his Tinder profile. We went to a small bar in Newtown where I downed several cocktails to alleviate my horrific date anxiety. The cocktails did their job fast and I ended up talking at him for several hours before convincing him to kick on with me at my favourite Mexican joint in the next suburb over.

Across a tray of chips and dips, I asked him about his relationship with his mum, his childhood and his greatest fears. His rejoinder was to ask, 'What do you think about pineapple on pizza?' I couldn't work out if he was taking the piss or if he just didn't like to get too deep on a first date, but whatever the reason I quickly realised I wasn't getting the vibe I'd been hoping for. I was out of practice and there was no producer to call time, so I just made out with him outside the restaurant until my Uber pulled up. We didn't have a second date.

Next was James. James was the Punkee Recap Guy. Punkee was a website aimed at young people that covered news and pop culture in an irreverent, cheeky way. James had become semi-famous for his quick-fire video recaps of *The Bachelor*, stuffed with memes, nostalgia and a considerable number of references to *Shrek*. I'd had a crush on him for ages and had been consistently flirting with him on Instagram. We had a date at a dumpling house in Haymarket and went back to his apartment.

Then there was my F45 trainer, whom I'd flirted with through an eight-week challenge. The flirting eventually moved from my six-thirty a.m. class to Instagram, where he started to invite me to house parties and knock-off drinks. I was really right in the middle of that late twenties transition where you start preferring moody wine bars and nine p.m. bedtimes to necking vodka lime sodas at a packed Bondi pub, but he was cute and insistent and I was trying to fill my nights lest I fall any deeper into my creeping depression.

He was twenty-one and the five-year age gap made me feel like Jennifer Coolidge, but my girlfriends told me to just chill and have some fun. I did try. I went to the drinks, danced at the house parties, crashed at his, but I couldn't escape the feeling that he was so much younger than me. It was like he spoke a different language. He'd reply to innocuous texts about making dinner with *'Sounds juicy'* or *'Extremely kinky'*. Eventually, I decided I might try running instead.

Lachlan was the one who broke me. Like James and David, he was a really nice guy, with nothing screamingly wrong with him at all. He was in the Labor Party, worked for a shadow minister and had worked in the media for about a decade before that. We sat for hours at a Surry Hills pub deep in interesting conversation. We talked about politics, reality TV, our values and what direction we hoped our lives were headed in. Like so many of these dates, I tried to find little sparks and things in common that meant we were destined for each other.

I wasn't delusional enough not to notice that the spark wasn't there, but I really wanted it to be. I was growing increasingly frustrated that the relationships that set my heart alight seemed to be those that were painful and chaotic. The ones that I didn't feel secure in.

So I really tried to make this thing with Lachlan happen, the way I'd tried to make David, James and the F45 trainer happen. We went for a brunch date the next week, with decidedly less conversation than our first date, and then I pushed for a third, inviting him over for pasta at my place. He arrived at six-thirty p.m. The pasta was already prepped. I plated it up and we sat cross-legged at my Ikea Lack coffee table. By now our conversation had evaporated entirely, sentences punctuated by the knowledge that this wasn't going anywhere. I ended up sleeping with him by seven p.m, not knowing how else to deal with the awkwardness.

When he left, I found an episode of the *Real Housewives of Sydney* on YouTube and cried big, silly tears over a scene where one of the housewives, Athena X, lies back on a leather couch to be guided through a past-life regression by a hypnotist. I was just exhausted. I thought I was doing all the right things. I was putting myself out there. I was being vulnerable. I had gone on two fucking TV shows.

When I wasn't feeling sorry for myself, I felt guilty about even wanting a partner. Every time I opened Instagram, I was greeted with another think-piece about embracing singledom, or needing to love myself before I could love anybody else. I knew there were women who were completely content being single but I wasn't one of them and I felt ashamed about it. I felt like I was expected to celebrate my independence and strength; if I didn't I was a failure, a bad feminist.

I'd been alone for so much of my life—without a sibling, without an invitation—and I didn't want to be alone anymore. I wanted someone to go through life with every day. I wanted companionship. My breathing finally started to slow as the scene changed to another two housewives—Matty and Christa—sipping champagne on the balcony of Christa's luxurious penthouse. I was all cried out but the heaviness didn't leave. I couldn't even muster a smile when Christa announced that her Pomeranian, Charlie, was getting married. To a cat. To promote marriage equality. *Good for them,* I thought. Even the Pomeranian had found somebody.

That heaviness wouldn't leave for a while. It became my new normal. While, outwardly, I tucked my ugly sadness away and continued holding court with the girls, trading stories about bad dates and bad sex over wine, each morning I was waking up feeling worse. My eyes would open, greeting another morning as uninspiring as the last. I'd think to myself, *Fuck—is this what we all do for the rest of our lives? We get up, we get dressed, we catch the train to work, we come home, then we do it all again.* I didn't want to get up. I didn't want to get dressed. I definitely did not want to catch the train to work.

At work, a group of union secretaries were in the process of replacing Kaila. The office had shrunk since the elections and the remaining staff could be counted on two hands. I don't know what I had expected after Kaila left, but I'd thought at the very least one of the senior members of the office would've gathered everyone together and given a pep talk of sorts. Maybe tell us everything was going to be fine, ask us what we were working on, check that we were all going okay. But there was nothing like that. Radio silence.

The silence was especially profound around me because there was a perception that I was loyal to Kaila. I couldn't just care about the Labor Party, or the work that I was doing, and it couldn't simply just be a friendship—there had to be darkness, shadows and dirty dealings. Loyalty was a threat, and threats were dealt with by isolation. From Kaila's resignation onward, it was basically a moot point whether or not I came into the office. No one checked in about what I was doing or whether I was even there.

Working in politics wasn't unlike the raft I'd built all those months ago with Daniel in *Paradise*. Things would start off okay, buoyed by a common goal and excitement that all your efforts were actually paying off. But then, slowly but surely, more and more water starts lapping at the wood. Uncertainty creeps in, and you can feel your weight putting pressure on the structure. Then everything compounds and it becomes clear that, despite your best efforts, the raft isn't really going to work out after all. People on the raft start to look for jobs in the private sector, maybe lobbying. If you fail to time your exit with enough thought and care, soon enough the sea will swallow you, along with your shitty arrangement of logs and rope.

I didn't want to be looking for an exit strategy, but I could feel the tide turning and each day grew more toxic. Staff in the office were hardly even bothering to minimise Seek when the hiring manager walked past. Everyone was just trying to find a crumb of joy, wherever possible. For me, it was starting to plan the office Christmas party. I was halfway paging through Google results for 'Inner West Free Venue Hire' when my phone buzzed with a familiar caller ID.

'Oh my god,' I said to the empty office. I laughed and picked up the phone with more animation than I'd displayed in months. It was Warner Brothers. It was an exit strategy.

Meg and I exchanged pleasantries and I told her how much I was enjoying the newest season of *The Bachelor*. The new Bachelor was a guy called Matt Agnew. He was smart, an astrophysicist. I joked that she'd cast me on the wrong season. We bantered back and forth about the series until she moved on to the purpose of the call, which I'd already happily intuited.

'What would you think about Fiji again?' she asked.

Before this moment, I hadn't given a thought to returning to *Bachelor in Paradise*. I'd felt like I'd peaked on the last season and, consciously or unconsciously, I'd been trying to acclimatise back to the nine-to-five: slowly building a career, ticking off all the things you're supposed to—a promotion here, a salary increase there. I really had felt like the reality TV chapter was closed and it was time to move on. I didn't want to be one of those people who kept rocking up to Fiji until they age out of the show like I'd aged out of Young Labor. But I think in my heart I knew I needed to get out of NSW Labor before I was swallowed whole, and what better way than a paid holiday to Fiji?

I told Meg that it wasn't a no. She asked if she could start the process, send over some preliminary casting documents: a questionnaire, a medical, the psych analysis. Again, it wasn't a no.

Meg's call planted a seed, and the next morning for the first time in weeks I didn't have to drag myself out of bed. I felt invigorated, like life was moving again. I didn't want to be dependent on this rhythm of phone calls from Warner Brothers to feel good and excited, but with work, life and love the way it was, I was looking for anything to lift me out of the sludge. I smiled at strangers on the train and powered through my workday, ringing every restaurant on King Street in Newtown to figure out which had the best set menu for the Christmas party, taking into consideration Labor's austere post-ICAC budget. On the way home, I splurged on a twenty-dollar bottle of rosé. I sat with Hannah on our small verandah, surrounded by the half-dead plants that we would definitely revive one day, and wrote out the pros and cons of doing another season of the show.

I kicked us off. 'Work fucking sucks.'

Hannah worked in the union movement, adjacent to politics, and was well aware of how uncomfortable the environment at NSW Labor had grown since the ICAC hearings. Throughout our twenties we had counselled each other through the ebbs and flows of our burgeoning careers and this was no different. We workshopped what would come next if not the show and agreed that I likely needed to find a way out of the office regardless. Hannah scribbled 'Paid holiday' in the pro column. Fiji could give me some breathing room to figure out what I wanted to do. I took a sip of my wine.

'What if I get booted really fast?'

She responded as any best friend would, gushing 'Babe, absolutely not,' and 'You'll be there for ages.' Hannah knew how it worked, though. *Bachelor in Paradise* had a much higher day rate than *The Bachelor*, which made doing the show very tempting. But if you didn't connect with someone and you were only there for a couple of days, you'd slink back home with a paltry amount to remunerate your rapid rejection. I guess that's why the producers bumped up the pay cheque for the spin-off; their pool of candidates was far too aware of the costs. They needed to balance it out with benefits. If I was to go back for a third season, I felt that it would have to be worth it. With Kaila gone, it was unclear whether I'd be able to keep my job if I was to do another season and while a couple of thousand dollars wasn't insignificant money, it also wasn't a lot for another full year on Warner Brothers' ferris wheel.

We both stared at the railway line across the road from the apartment building and listened to a train rumble past.

'What if you meet someone?'

I sat with the question for a moment, remembering running on the beach. Stamping my feet against the sand, so twisted up with hurt and rejection, but also so alive. I rolled my eyes theatrically at Hannah and wrote down 'Might meet someone' in the pro column and 'Probably won't' with the cons. I underscored 'won't' twice and sculled the last of my wine.

'I do like the idea of my *Bachelor* journey not being defined by Jules though,' I said to Hannah. 'I don't want to look back in twenty, thirty years' time and it just be this whole sad thing that centred on one guy.'

'Don't get them to fly me over to meet anyone else though. One season was enough for me, thanks,' she said.

I laughed and poured us another glass.

Over the next couple of weeks, I went back and forth on calls with Meg and Marti, figuring out whether I'd end up in Fiji.

Meg dangled a carrot, saying that Warner Brothers was looking to cast some people particularly for me, and I should send her an email describing the type of person I was looking for. I'm sure it was less an offer of genuine matchmaking from the casting director and more soft manipulation to make me excited about doing it all again. If I met someone in *Paradise* once, who was to say it couldn't happen again?

The tactic worked. I sent her some dot points under the subject line 'Dream Guy', prefacing it with the warning that it was all pretty standard stuff: funny, intelligent, looking for something serious, not too straighty one-eighty, but not out on a bender every weekend.

'Jules, but emotionally available and maybe a little older and maybe even slightly more nerdy, if you know of this perfect man.'

She replied five minutes later. 'Leave this with me. As I have said before, we like to think our stats are pretty good, so you never know what/who we can find. Let's talk at the end of this week.'

Marti also rang about the money. I'd heard on the grapevine about deals other cast members had negotiated with production over the years. Rumour had it that Richie and Alex were paid 4000 dollars per day for their appearance on the last season. That was the kind of money I couldn't even fathom. The perception that from the moment someone appears on reality TV they are rich and famous couldn't be further from the truth, as I quickly learnt after my first season. While I'd finally scored some invitations to parties after *Bachelor in Paradise* aired, I still hadn't monetised my appearance any further than 500 dollars I'd scored from an Instagram collaboration with Destination NSW to promote Sydney's lights and arts festival Vivid. I'd struggled to even secure that because I didn't really have an understanding of how the whole influencer economy, filled with agencies and PR firms, worked. I'd made my friend Dylan, the then Digital Organiser at NSW Labor, help me set up an email address for a fake talent manager, at a fake influencer agency called Punch Communications. 'Elliott' from Punch Communications negotiated anything that arrived in my inbox for about four months. He wasn't very good though—he couldn't even land a deal with HelloFresh.

Growing up without a stable or consistent family income—and at times, during my childhood, just trying to survive—had made me very attached to the security that came with money and by extension, the security of a full-time job. I wasn't earning a huge salary but I can't understate the reassurance I felt knowing that a pay cheque of the same size would arrive in my bank account each fortnight. Doing another season meant uncertainty, and uncertainty was anathema to safety.

I asked for guaranteed payment for fourteen days. Hannah and I had roughly sketched out the numbers on the bottom of the pros and cons list. I punched figures into the calculator on my iPhone, and once I'd landed somewhere I felt was reasonable, I scribbled it on the page, underlining it three times before looking up at Hannah. There it was, the sweet spot, the number that balanced out the risk to my career, potential embarrassment and potential heartbreak. Everyone has a price.

I went back and forth with Marti, whom, I quickly discovered, was a fastidious negotiator. I would have a call with Marti and then debrief with Hannah. In each debrief with Hannah it became clearer that I was not in a position of power.

I'd gotten too excited. Meg was good at her job and now instead of focusing on the pay, I was fantasising about who might be waiting for me in Fiji. It was like the contract renegotiation scene in *30 Rock*: Liz Lemon and Jack Donaghy are meeting with NBC's talent, Josh Girard, and his agent in Donaghy's office. Liz and Jack sit in high leather chairs while Jack and his agent sink into what are basically beanbags. Liz asks Jack what the go was with the new furniture, to which he replies, 'It's my negotiation set.' I was in the beanbag.

Marti and I met somewhere in the middle and my signature ended up on a contract to join *Bachelor in Paradise* for a second time. I didn't tell my boss until after the deal was done this time. Thankfully the ever-revolving door at NSW Labor worked in my favour. Kaila still hadn't been replaced and my interim boss was about to leave for a new role himself. He didn't care what I did with myself, or how much leave I needed to take. He told me to have fun and drink a margarita for him. I politely obliged.

When I got back to my office, a familiar cast questionnaire was sitting in my inbox.

'What are you most looking forward to about Bachelor in Paradise?'

'Meeting new people and having new experiences. I really enjoyed my first round of *Paradise* (despite the heartbreak) and there's still a bit of me that hopes I could get my little Bach fantasy and round off my experience by meeting someone who could actually be my future.'

'What are your biggest turn-ons?'

'Treating women with respect and bringing me a coffee when I'm hungover.'

'Why do you think you're still single?'

'I just think I haven't bumped into the right person yet. I just haven't found "The One".'

I checked over the answers and attached the document to the email.

Send.

CHAPTER 8

Third Time Lucky

I was due to fly back to Fiji on 9 November. I had a feeling it wasn't the first fly-out date for the cast, meaning I'd enter the show as an intruder, and this was quickly confirmed by the forums. Checking the forums had become a daily habit again, even before a second season of *Bachelor in Paradise* was on the table. The habit had become so ingrained that sometimes I found myself unconsciously typing out the first few words of the forum's title in the URL bar until my phone predicted what I wanted to see and loaded up the page. About a week before my flight was scheduled, a user uploaded photos of Abbie

Chatfield and Brittney Weldon at the Fiji Airways counter with a Warner Brothers minder.

The forums had been speculating about the potential cast for months. It was mostly new names from the latest seasons of *The Bachelor* and *The Bachelorette*. I felt old and out of the loop and forced myself to get up to speed on the tangled web of relationships between them. One of the frontrunners from *The Bachelorette*, Ciarran, had previously dated one of the contestants on *The Bachelor*, Renee. Bobette predicted they would end up on the show together.

This was new territory for me. While plenty of contestants had dated people from the show, the relationships were usually established after filming, they weren't pre-existing. I felt cynical about the whole thing—it seemed like pre-gaming on a whole new level: pre-producing a storyline to hand to producers on a platter. Last year had been so turbulent, I think I resented people being cast who didn't have to build their relationships from scratch. To me, it pushed the boundaries of allowable performativity on the show. It felt like they were cheating.

I gathered as much intel as possible before my flight, and by the time I got to the airport, any trepidation had been replaced with anticipation. I found comfort in the familiarity of getting ready for Fiji. Making sure I sent Hannah a bunch of generic pictures and accompanying captions so she could keep my

Instagram active while I was away. Packing my two suitcases and pulling out the black hoodie they'd given me all the way back in my first season of *The Bachelor* to abide by Warner Brothers' instructions to look inconspicuous. I even enjoyed the three-hour drive to the Naviti. This time I'd planned ahead and bought a new iPod for the drive, for fear I'd have to listen to unsolicited U2 again. A guy called Mohammed had listed the sixth-generation iPod Classic on Facebook Marketplace for the bargain price of fifty dollars and I'd driven to Kings Cross the night before my flight to collect it. I hadn't had a chance to update the songs before I left, which I only realised fifteen minutes into our drive through the streets of Nadi. Thankfully, amid Mohammed's eclectic catalogue of Bollywood hits and country favourites, I found we had a shared love for The Killers and relaxed back into the sticky leather seats as we cut through the rolling hills of the lush Fijian countryside, 'Mr Brightside' blaring.

I took a deep breath when we arrived. The fresh air mixed with that very specific chlorinated smell of the pool at family-friendly resorts. Every little detail made me feel like I'd made the right decision. I was back in an experience I enjoyed so much and this time I felt like I was reclaiming it for myself.

It was the best sensation in the world, to belong. When you've been around certain people, or done a certain thing, for so long, you've successfully traversed all the awkwardness and discomfort and one day you discover that you feel at home. Because I was entering the show late, I wasn't sharing a room with anyone at the Naviti and over the forty-eight hours of my sequester, Warner Brothers staff streamed in and out of my room, popping in for a chat, telling me they were so happy to see me back.

The night before I was due to enter *Paradise*, my room became the unofficial meeting place for production. I sat around with Pip from wardrobe, Lisa from admin and Alex, my beloved psych, chatting about all the shows they'd worked on since I'd seen them last and pressing them for details about what had happened in *Paradise* so far. I teased Alex the most, asking her if my future husband was there, knowing she would give nothing away, until her phone rang, loudly interrupting our conversation. She walked into the doorway to try to take the call in confidence but the room was small and her voice carried. It was clear she was needed on set. She made a speedy goodbye, failing to mask the urgency. It was rare that a psychologist was called onto set from the Naviti: sometimes a cast member might request a call, or they'd arrange a meeting in the morning, but an intervention during shooting virtually never happened.

It made me both intrigued and anxious about what I'd be walking into. I'd soon learn that the night had turned to chaos because Renee had in fact rocked up, as predicted by the forum sleuths, but instead of arriving to a romantic reunion with her ex, she'd arrived to find Ciarran in a range of new relationships. The simmering tension had boiled over during a 'Bula Banquet', a new feature of the third season. The banquets involved the cast reading out and responding to anonymous questions, all of which, that particular night, had focused on Ciarran and Renee's romantic history.

As a result, *Paradise* was fairly melancholy by the time I entered the next day. It turned out Alex had averted multiple early exits from the show the previous night and counselled more than a couple of contestants through their tears. It was so quiet when I walked down the familiar path in front of the bures that I almost thought nobody was going to say hello. Thankfully, two people were sitting close to the entry, with their legs dangling off a small embankment above the beach. They clocked my excited squeal and jumped up to greet me.

One was Cassandra Mamone. I'd watched her on the last season of *The Bachelor*. The other was Glenn Smith. He was from the last season of *The Bachelorette*. Someone else might not have recognised him, but I was a student of the show. Glenn, 32, Refrigeration Mechanic, Perth. That's what would have come up on the lower-third of the screen if he'd had any screen time at all, but he hadn't, so I'd only learnt his name by stalking the contestant profiles on the Channel Ten website. Glenn was really good-looking. Like, *really* good-looking. The type of guy I would generally never approach, or consider, or date, because I assumed that if you were that good-looking you had to be an asshole. He greeted me with a warm hug, as did Cass, and they accompanied me into *Paradise* for my second time.

Naturally, I found my way to the bar and the girls, and requested the story so far. Two of my new castmates, Mary Viturino and Jessica Brody, took turns fielding my questions, while I balanced a margarita in my hand. I prided myself on feeling my way through *Paradise* according to my intuition, so I opened the conversation with a specific inquiry.

'Tell me someone's not with Glenn,' I said. It felt bizarre to even consider, but there had been some sort of immediacy when we'd met. It wasn't frenzied chemistry, like I'd felt before. It was softer. It was in the way he held my eye contact and how he'd so confidently wrapped his arms around me.

Mary responded that he was a hot commodity. He had a little something going on with Helena Sauzier, also from the west coast. They hadn't been on a formal date, but they had been flirting. It was just as Mary admitted that she'd been flirting with Glenn too that Osher arrived and announced he was taking me back out of *Paradise*, before I'd even gotten comfortable. Osher and I stopped at a staging area just outside the main set. As he spoke, everything clicked into place. Osher told me I was going to be meeting three new men, who had never featured on *The Bachelor* franchise before. These were Meg's promised guys. Men apparently cast particularly for me. Instead of being irritated at being pulled out of *Paradise* I was suddenly intrigued. I was surprised they actually delivered and couldn't have been more eager to see what Warner Brothers' Cupid would bring me.

When I met the guys, I immediately understood the rationale for casting each of them. There was Conor, a serious real estate agent from Tasmania, who told me he'd spent too much of his twenties concentrating on his business and was ready to concentrate on finding love.

Next was Gilly, from Geraldton, another west coast boy. Gilly was warm and charismatic; he felt a bit like Jules *sans* soft boi energy.

Last was Tim. He was hot. He couldn't really hold a conversation and didn't ask me anything about myself but he looked really good while talking about himself.

They all had something uniquely attractive but I wanted it all rolled into one. I didn't feel a romantic connection with any of them and I felt a little bit guilty that Meg's creative casting was seemingly a bust.

I knew the girls would be happy though. Even from a mathematical perspective alone, it meant that there were now two more men than women, so the women would have the power at the next rose ceremony. I returned to *Paradise* jubilant, with the three guys arranged around me.

Everyone scattered as soon as we arrived, the new faces to get to know the rest of the cast and the men who'd been there a while to do some work, given the changed power dynamics. I parked myself at the bar and chatted to a *Paradise* veteran, Jake Ellis, who had fallen in love on the first season, but it hadn't worked out. Jake and I were having very different experiences: where I had growing confidence in my decision to come back, Jake had regrets.

It was the little things: the pillows on the day beds or the wood carvings on the wall. Remembering a conversation you'd had at the bar, or on the lounges. Seeing where you'd first kissed. I knew how he felt but thanks to the excitement of the first day my nostalgia was still buried. Jake was feeling raw and was halfway through explaining his disappointment that no one had leapt out at him, when I rudely interrupted.

'Do you know who's leapt out at me?'

'Who?' Jake responded.

'Glenn,' I told him coyly.

Jake was kind enough to indulge my bait-and-switch, and laughed, telling me that Glenn was a nice guy and that I should go and talk to him. But I was nervous. Today had felt a lot like primary school, when frantic whispers about who had a crush on whom had whipped around the playground.

I was reminded of walking home from school through the suburban streets of Lane Cove West with my Year 6 crush. I'd been prodding him for weeks to tell me who he liked. We'd stopped at the intersection where our paths diverged when he'd said he'd only tell me the person's initials. He'd gotten into a sprinter's crouching start on the footpath, yelled 'AAR' and pelted away. I'd floated the rest of the way home.

But this time I was in the same position as my crush, so nervous about putting something into motion that I was almost tempted to sprint away. With Jake's encouragement, I stood and headed towards the group of men Glenn was talking to, asking to steal him away.

Glenn and I sat exactly where I'd first spoken to Jules, almost a year ago to the day. I couldn't quite believe that I was here again and I definitely couldn't believe that I felt such attraction again. I'd always thought real emotions were a rarity on reality TV and yet lightning had struck twice.

I decided to put it all out there. If my experience with Jules had taught me anything, it was that rejection could come anytime—there was no protection in being indirect. I told Glenn that I felt nervous but that I'd felt instantly connected to him when I'd walked in. He instantly matched my openness. We stuttered over each other's words and anxious laughter, dancing between syllables as both of us tried to craft a full sentence.

'I'll be completely honest as well,' he told me. He said he thought that there had been an immediate mutual attraction.

I was floating again; back in primary school, buoyed by a mutual crush. It was so refreshing to be volunteering exactly how we felt about each other, to talk about the spark so openly, with no power dynamics, no games. It was just a conversation.

We talked about his dating history, his experience on *The Bachelor* and how he'd been finding his *Paradise* experience so far. He mentioned he'd been hanging out with Helena, but nothing had really progressed. I said 'Cool' under my breath and quickly apologised for it, realising it was a slightly too enthusiastic response.

Then I called him the wrong name.

I'd gone pedal to the metal with the admissions and told him that I'd been talking to Mary about how attractive I thought he was. 'Mary, I'm hot for Greg,' I recollected, so confidently, so casually. *Greg.* I'd called him Greg. He politely corrected me. I was mortified, but he found it funny. It was a stark reminder that despite the flowing conversation and our shared attraction, we had only met five hours ago.

He told me he was glad I was here. I told him it was good to be back and we closed our conversation with a cheers.

It *was* good to be back. I felt comfortable on set, back with crew members that I'd met all the way back on my first season of *The Bachelor*. Hot Tom, Dean, Laura, Marti. I felt like I was back with my family, with people who embraced every bit of my personality.

I loved the rhythm of the days. A long black from Tina who worked at the resort, a few kettlebell squats to fit in with the cast members who couldn't miss their daily workout, then putting on our microphones by ten a.m.

I felt at home when a producer prompted me to sit on the swinging day bed, as he attempted to set up a scene with a bunch of girls to discuss the events of the night before. I sat with three of my castmates unpacking where we were all at. When the conversation shifted to Glenn, the girls gave rave reviews.

'Glenn is just, like, the nicest human,' one girl said.

'I feel like he is the most eligible bachelor here,' another continued.

I was so used to my friends finding my choice of partner questionable that I felt a sense of pride when the girls spoke so highly of him.

'I very rarely have sexual chemistry with someone,' I told them. 'It doesn't usually happen for me like that.'

In fact, it never happened for me like that. In my early twenties, I had described myself as a sapiosexual, a word I think many women latch on to when they first discover it. It sounds reasonable enough—intelligence is attractive, after all—except that I think I was using that word because I really just hadn't had very many good sexual experiences, so sex was never at the forefront of my mind. When I did develop feelings for someone, it was generally based on our conversation or their personality.

Back when I'd first started dating, I'd sometimes date people just because they were persistent. They wanted me and I liked being wanted. It felt different to have such a strong physical attraction to someone straightaway. I'd never wanted to 'jump someone's bones' before, as I told the girls. But I did want to jump Glenn's bones.

What I didn't tell them was how exposed that made me feel.

For quite a bit of my life, I'd just assumed I was broken. That something was a bit off. Growing up, everything I read or watched seemed to put sex up on a pedestal, as one of the most exciting, mind-blowing things in life. Whether it was *American Pie*, or *Sex and the City*, or the adult chat rooms I'd log on to as a teenager when Mum wasn't home, it seemed like everyone was either talking about sex, thinking about sex or having sex.

Which is why I was so confused when I eventually had it. *This is what everyone had been raving about?* I felt like I was missing something.

My 'first time' had been in the attic of my boyfriend's family home. We'd been dating for about eight months and we had sex a couple of months after my sixteenth birthday because I was a rule-follower and insistent that we wait until it was legal. We decided we should do it on his carpeted floor in case his mum came home and heard us.

It wasn't great. Neither of us really knew what lubricant was and I definitely wasn't particularly turned on by staring up at his bookshelves stacked with copies of the Artemis Fowl series. It was short, it was painful and it didn't leave me with the feeling of wanting to do it again anytime soon. I just couldn't understand that this was the thing that had been built up in my mind for so many years. That this thing seemed to be the centre of every single story.

It didn't get much better either. Throughout my late teens and early twenties I had sex with people mostly just to get to the cuddling. I wanted the intimacy, to be held in the arms of the person I liked, and sex was just a vehicle to get there. I faked orgasms with basically every partner I had until I was twenty-six because after ten minutes I just wanted the whole thing to be over.

I'd read articles online about communication being the key to good sex but that had always felt a little bit awkward to me. None of the guys that I'd slept with had ever asked me what I liked or what felt good—there was no dialogue at all. I guess I felt at the time that if I said anything I'd be ruining the mood, or being burdensome, so I'd just stuck with my routine of making sure they had a great time and acting like I'd had one too.

As I got older, I did get better at asking for what I wanted, or saying that something wasn't working for me, but good sex was still so rare and I knew deep down that I was still being driven by a want for intimacy than any pleasure for myself. The whole idea of being so physically attracted to someone from the start was strangely intimidating. The stakes seemed so much higher.

Just as my chat with the girls wrapped up, Mary danced into *Paradise* with an arm in the air, presenting a date card. It was revealed to be for career-orientated Conor and he had chosen Britt Weldon to go on the date with him—her first date in three seasons.

Unfortunately for Britt, the delivery of the date card coincided with a spate of bad gastro through the cast. Britt was struck first, just as she headed back to her bure to get ready for the date. The medic on staff told her she'd need to be isolated until she felt better, to protect the rest of *Paradise*.

Glenn, seeing a date up for grabs, decided to speak to the producers about us using it instead. Apparently Conor didn't mind, so they were out, we were in—and there was a driver waiting for us.

We travelled back to the Naviti, where a wooden balcony outside the Cantonese restaurant on-site had been transformed into the set of our date. The headrests of the driver's and passenger's seats had GoPros affixed to them, capturing what was happening in the back seat. Producer Laura travelled with us. She twisted to turn the cameras on and clapped so post-production would be able to sync the audio and video.

There were moments on *Bachelor in Paradise* when the cameras faded away, but this was not one of them. I felt self-conscious about the twenty-minute drive in a small car with Laura in the front, thinking she'd be judging our vibe or my attempts at flirtation. I slipped into the safety of performance and kept the conversation light, fixed on the structure of the show. That felt easy, I was comfortable there. I posited to Glenn that given there were now more men than women in *Paradise*, he might have just been pursuing me to lock down a rose at the next rose ceremony.

He turned to me and returned serve. 'I think by the end of the day you'll figure that out yourself. If I'm here for a rose or something more,' he replied.

I bit my fist. 'That is so hot.'

Laura and I looked at each other. She mouthed 'Wow!' and I adjusted myself in my seat. Glenn was so forthright that it almost made me uncomfortable.

When we arrived, we were greeted by a beauty therapist, likely recruited from the hotel, who announced that we'd be having a banana leaf massage. She wouldn't be massaging us—we would be responsible for the lathering up part. She gestured to a rattan benchtop packed with various body butters, lotions and oils.

I always felt bad for the third party on *Bachelor* dates. You'd inevitably see them awkwardly positioned in the back of the shot while the two people on the date ended up making out for an inordinate period of time. They always looked supremely unimpressed, no doubt questioning every life choice that had brought them to this point. Thankfully, our therapist was spared an extended cameo and she left us to our own devices.

No further prompting was required by the producers; we both understood the assignment.

'Do I take my skirt off?' I asked Glenn.

'I don't think it's going to be appropriate to be wearing clothes with all this . . .'

'Body butter,' I finished his sentence.

We both laughed. I was grateful we matched each other's energy. A crew of four watched on as we scooped out big globs of body butter and proceeded to rub it across each other's chests and arms. One of the camera operators, who took his cinematography seriously, requested that we hold briefly while he switched modes to shoot in slow motion.

He gestured Glenn towards one of the bottles of body oil. 'I think that will look really good, mate,' he directed, with a seriousness that was endearing, given the setting.

Glenn joyfully complied and poured the oil onto my bikini top, only interrupted by the camera operator returning to encourage him to play with the height of the bottle.

Once Spielberg had gotten his shot, we returned to the 'massage'. While Glenn rubbed massage oil onto my face like a dad brusquely applying sunscreen to his kid, I was waiting for a kiss. I'd wanted to kiss him since our very first conversation, but despite my many signals, he wasn't picking up what I was putting down. I had to fall back on a classic move: 'Let me get this,' I said, as I brushed his cheek with my hand before going in for a kiss. The chemistry only increased.

After the kiss, the therapist returned to help wrap us in large banana leaves that were arranged on the floor. We waited, making small talk with the producers, while an overhead camera was erected above them. Laura prompted us to return to relevant *Paradise* topics and we obliged.

'I'm oiled up, in a banana leaf, with a really good-looking guy. Is this not *Paradise*?' I said.

'This is *Paradise*. I was taken the moment you walked in,' Glenn said. 'I knew I had to do something to catch your attention.'

That earnest tone was back again and something in it made me cringe. I thought he was claiming to have somehow set up the date we were on, rather than just asking the producers if he could take Conor's. He hadn't been, but I started to spiral. I thought I had been largely unaffected by the year before, but between that and the intensity with which this thing with Glenn had begun, my spiral continued.

On the way back from the date, with the GoPros off, we delved more into our lives back in Sydney and Perth. I told him about politics and why I had joined the Labor Party. He told me about his air-conditioning business and the work he did with local charities. He told me about a mentoring program he was involved in, working with primary-school students to help them build self-esteem, and a collective giving program he contributed to each year that had helped the PCYC start up a breakfast club for local kids.

I felt guilty that my first reaction when he'd mentioned the word charity was cynicism. I'd assumed he was virtue signalling, pretending like he cared about the same things that I did. Not only was it a shitty thought to have, but my reaction had also undeservedly elevated my own altruism.

But I couldn't help myself. I was on the hunt for red flags, looking for warnings against giving over my heart more fully. He was too kind, too quiet, too absolute. I kept telling myself that there was something wrong. That there was something that meant he wasn't right for me.

I was slipping into the same place Jake Ellis was. The pillows on the day beds and the wood carvings on the wall were suddenly screaming at me. *You had something before. You can't find it again. It will end the same way.*

But all the red lights kept coming up green. I had been too quick to decide I knew exactly who he was. I'd actually done the same thing with Jules. I was too preoccupied with the vision I'd created in my mind, which was why I was always so disappointed in the end. Glenn wasn't wokefishing me, he was just trying to share part of his world. He was quiet, but it wasn't because he wasn't interested, or wasn't engaged. He just didn't feel the need to be the loudest person in the room or to fill every silence like I did. And he was absolute, but that clarity was all I'd been asking for the last time I'd been in *Paradise*. And now when I had it, I was suddenly willing it away.

When I allowed him to show me who he actually was, instead of constructing a narrative around him, I discovered he was exactly who I'd been looking for. It shone through in ways he wouldn't have even realised. Like the way he talked about his ex-girlfriend, whom he'd dated for eight years in his twenties. I was glad that he'd dated someone before me and that it had been such a long love.

When I was younger, I would have bristled at the idea of a partner being in love with someone else before me. I had to be their one great love; if they'd loved someone before me, we were obviously not destined to be.

But when Glenn told me about their life together—their travels and their border collie, Bindi—instead of feeling insecure, I felt even more attracted to him. He spoke of her with reverence, as an important part of his life and his story. And when he shared with me that they'd seen a therapist towards the end of their relationship, it was one of the best signs of all. I imagined asking my most recent ex, The One, to see a therapist with me. He would have laughed in my face.

Over conversations on the day beds dotted around *Paradise*, we traded stories of first loves, bad loves, our first times and our worst times. He told me about his mum, Noeleen, and his dad, Graham. They had been together for forty-eight years.

I divulged I was jealous of parental love stories and told him about my difficult relationship with my dad.

He told me about his twin brother Neil. That he'd just met a new guy, called Marty, and Marty had come over for dinner a couple of times before Glenn had left for Fiji. Glenn said that he'd never seen his brother more in love.

While the show whirred around us, we took these moments in each day to build a foundation. Not of obsession or fixation, but of interest and exploration.

Paradise had been changing quickly since our body butter date. Conor had connected with Mary and they'd been going on long beach walks every morning. A guy called Matt from Glenn's season had arrived and quickly shifted an existing friendship with Renee into something more. Ciarran was into his third relationship in three weeks, with a woman called Kiki that he had also been connected to before the show. And there was someone new for Britt Weldon too: Jackson Garlick, a rugby league player and heir to one of Australia's biggest pie brands, Garlo's Pies. Jackson was a good time and beloved among the boys.

Alcohol politics in *Paradise* was funny. The bar opened at midday, and they policed our allotted two drinks an hour relatively well, putting tally marks next to our names in a big ruled notepad each time we came to collect a drink. The cast had a theory that the cocktails were watered down and the brand of beer they served tasted like Mount Franklin so we'd all end up drinking red wine with ice cubes during the balmy afternoons.

Everyone was in good spirits the day after Jackson's arrival and you could feel the bubbling excitement that suggested a rowdy night to come celebrating our new arrivals. We ordered round after round of red wine and perched beside the pool, listening to our resident storyteller Jamie Doran tell highly detailed accounts of his travels around the world or watching castmates prepare and perform synchronised swimming routines of varying skill.

On days like these, when the producers were trying to catch up on our individual interviews, we were mostly left to our own devices. Jackson and I had started to talk politics. I told him about student politics and the Labor Party and the chants we'd sing as we marched down George Street protesting against the Liberal Government. The red wine was starting to catch up with me, and ten minutes later I was leaning back on the padded tropical couch, holding up my wine, yelling, 'Jackson Garlick, get out, we know what you're all about. Cuts, job losses, money for the bosses.'

The boys found it hysterical. They put their own spins on it, and we laughed as they tested them out.

I rolled out another. 'What do we want? Glenn Smith! When do we want it? Now!'

They liked that one even more.

The afternoon descended into a blur of banter and belligerence. One of the head producers, returning from hours in the humid huts we interviewed in, was unimpressed with the scene. We were like kids denying that we'd eaten the chocolate but caught with it smeared all over our faces: our mouths and teeth were stained red and there was more than one plastic pina colada glass floating in the pool. Production wasn't happy.

'How did you manage this?' the producer scolded. 'We can't use any of this footage, you all look like disasters,' he informed us. Shooting was off for the night; they'd pick it up again tomorrow.

I woke up with a dull headache. I didn't want to open my eyes, and my mouth felt dry and metallic. Too much red wine. Glenn's arm was draped heavily across me, hugging my stomach, and I was all of five centimetres away from toppling out of the single bed onto the floor of the bure.

He'd spent the night for the first time. I'd slurred that we were only going to cuddle, my attempt to protect my heart from what I now thought of as last year's missteps.

'Morning, beautiful,' he said.

I patted his hand in reply, trying to communicate my hang-over without the hard work of words. I whispered that I was going to get into the shower and stumbled heavily towards the door. There was no hot water—there was never any hot water—but it was fine this morning with the sun beaming down and my hangover dissipating with every cold drop. I tipped my head back into the water flowing from the shower and thought back to my earliest relationships. To my most challenging relationships. I thought about how empty I'd felt when I was newly single in Paris. I'd thought I was upset because I was alone, but now I realised I'd been upset because I'd been hurt. Love had been hurtful, chaotic. All the relationships that I'd thought had been what real love felt like had been marked by pain: by me thinking I wasn't cool enough, pretty enough, deserving enough.

This felt different. It felt calm, stable, secure. As the water ran over my face and through my hair, I decided that this would be a turning point: I would give myself over to the experience fully. Openness was in my nature, but until this point I hadn't really allowed it to show. I wasn't used to being that way in love. I decided I would let my guard down. I decided I deserved this.

I turned the water off, wrapped my towel around me and headed back into the room. Glenn was sitting on the bed with a long black for me. I really, really liked him.

Bit by bit, Glenn started to pull me out of the hole of overthinking and overanalysing, and helped me forget my heavy memories of the season before that I thought I'd been unaffected by.

Glenn was giving me what Jules never had: he was showing me that he wanted me one hundred per cent. I was one hundred per cent 'his Alisha'. I kept waiting for the beat where it was all going to fall apart. When someone would walk in and he would drop me in an instant, or when he'd decide I was 'too keen', and our mutual attraction would suddenly become unbalanced and unrequited.

It never happened.

Instead, we discussed what would happen after *Paradise*. What this might look like in the 'real world'. Naturally, being a reality TV show, these conversations took place on a paddleboard in the South Pacific Ocean. I lived in Sydney. He lived in Perth. We lived 3290 kilometres away from each other. Glenn's hands cut through the crystal water as he paddled us into the centre of the bay. I sat cross-legged on the back of the paddleboard. I told him I liked Perth, and when I visited I was determined to go to Dome and Gnomesville.

He laughed. 'How do you know about Gnomesville?' he asked. 'And nobody wants to go to Dome,' he added.

I reminded him that my ex-boyfriend Tom lived in Perth too. Tom's old boss had sent me a photo of their premier, Mark McGowan, surrounded by thousands of little gnomes. The collection was a tourist attraction around three hours south of Perth. I insisted we go.

'That doesn't explain why you want to go to Dome though,' Glenn said. It was a chain exclusive to the west coast where I'd had really excellent eggs Benedict. I hadn't had any to beat it since.

'Eggs Benny and Gnomesville it is,' Glenn promised. There was no question about whether or not I would be visiting Perth.

By the time we got to the now-familiar 'meeting the family and friends' beat of the season, I felt incredibly confident about us. There was no doubt that we were going to introduce each other to our loved ones.

Though she hadn't said anything explicitly, I knew that Mum had been disappointed that she hadn't been the one flown to Fiji to support me the first time. But when producers sat me down to discuss from a shortlist who would be best to bring over, Mum just hadn't been the right choice. Jules was a problem to be unpacked with a girlfriend, not a prospective partner to be introduced to your mum.

This year, Mum was on her way, and I was driven to an eco-resort deep in the Fijian hinterland. Each couple met their family and friends at different locations so the crew had divided to shoot two couples one day, and the other two the next.

Production made sure that each meeting had a clear theme. For Ciarran and Kiki, it was an interrogation over his multiple relationships. For Renee and Matt, an examination of whether she was truly over her ex. For Mary and Conor, a discussion about whether he was ready to be a stepfather to Mary's daughter Chanel. The theme for Glenn and I was whether we were too good to be true.

In the final edit, clips from my talking head interview prefaced the meetings. 'I have this all-consuming fear that I've gotten caught up in the fantasy,' I narrated. 'That this perfect bubble is one day going to burst.'

The seed for the theme had been planted on the morning of the meetings by producer Laura. The same Laura who had placated me nearly a year ago to the day, encouraging me to push on with Jules even though he was giving me nothing.

A make-up artist hovered around my face while Laura and I talked. Glenn and I feeling 'too perfect' was the only thread we consistently came back to, so that naturally became the anchor point of her interviews throughout the day. After a last mist of setting spray, the make-up artist relinquished me to production and Laura and I walked down to the long beach that wrapped around the resort.

The crew had set up just metres from the water and I tried to look natural while sitting on a big piece of driftwood, waiting for Mum to arrive. I was nervous about how she would handle the whole thing—there was generally an adjustment period to having multiple cameras in your face—but there'd been no need to worry. She was a natural. She wafted across the beach in a gorgeous floral dress, like she should've been the Bachelorette herself.

'So, you've met someone?' she inquired, as we tried to get comfortable on the driftwood.

'Who do you think it is?' I asked.

'Well . . . I was thinking Glenn,' Mum replied.

I could not believe it. I didn't generally believe in fate but this felt beyond spooky. I broke the fourth wall, mouthing 'Stop it!' to the camera man and audio guy, who were equally surprised—I was sure she must have heard something over a walkie-talkie or seen something on one of the producers' headshot sheets but she swore black and blue that she hadn't. She'd just picked him out of the line-up when she was looking at a group picture of Angie's season of *The Bachelorette*, knowing that those would be the bulk of the men that would end up cast for *Paradise*.

After only ten minutes, we were herded to a different section of the resort to meet Glenn and his twin brother Neil. I gripped her hand tightly as we walked towards them. I hadn't prepared her for the fact that Glenn and Neil were basically identical. I don't think I was quite prepared for how similar they were either. I had to double-check I wasn't being too affectionate with the wrong brother.

The whole day felt different to the year before, so much more comfortable, so much more mature. There was no ambiguity around whether he liked me, just some discussion about how the practicalities of our relationship would work.

We breezed through the 'final date' portion that had been so fraught last year. It felt as if we were moving in unison, like Glenn could sense that I just wanted to hurry through this particular checkpoint as fast as possible. We sat on the couch, popped our champagne, and gave the producers the lines they needed to progress our story for the audience. Once they felt they had enough material, we stopped shooting for the night and they let us head off to the moment I was truly interested in: tonight would be our first night together with no cameras, no audio, no surveillance. Just us. We left the set to a chorus of catcalls and winks. Our minder Palmer told us to have fun and stay safe.

When we opened the door to our room for the night, we saw that the producers had placed the cheeseboard we'd barely touched on a wooden table just across from the bed. Next to the cheeseboard was a comically large bowl of condoms. There would have been about twenty in there. We burst into laughter.

'Looks like we're in for a busy night,' Glenn declared.

We didn't sleep together straightaway, instead we picked at the fruit on the cheeseboard, which we'd moved to the bed, while saying all the things we hadn't been able to say while surveilled by production.

I asked him how he really felt about the experience. He said he was so glad he came. I pried into what he thought more generally about reality TV, referencing other contestants and shows to see how interested he was in celebrity. But his knowledge was rudimentary, to say the least, and what he did know was in relation to other guys in his cast who had already networked their way around the community. I asked him if he knew Bobette; he asked me if they were someone from *Married at First Sight*.

I ended my interrogation by asking if he really liked me, and he stood up to return the cheeseboard to the table. When he came back to the bed, he placed his hands on my hips, leaning in slowly to kiss me.

'You know how I feel about you and I know how you feel about me,' he said as he pulled away. After that, it was on. It wasn't like the movies and it wasn't like most of the previous sex I'd had, which had always felt obligatory, or as if we were sprinting towards his orgasm. Instead, we took it slow, some-times stopping to laugh when we got tangled, and sometimes completely quiet, our senses drowned in each other. A couple of minutes in, he paused and asked me to show him what I liked. With that question alone, it was already some of the best sex I'd ever had. We fell asleep at two a.m., cuddled tightly together, like we were still in our single bed in *Paradise*.

In the morning, we wandered down to the same beach I'd sat on with Mum. The water was as smooth as glass and the sun was still rising. We spoke about the commitment ceremony. At this point it felt like it was more for the producers than for us. But we were excited all the same. It was so novel to be the people standing at the end, to be the subject of all the pageantry the producers laid on. I told him they'd hired helicopters to fly the couples in last year and I was pissed that I'd just missed out. We also knew that there was an option to offer each other commitment rings but speculated about how it all worked, were they pre-allocated? Or did you get to choose? Glenn joked that I was getting ahead of myself. When we said goodbye to each other later that day, I joked that he'd better bring his best material.

We didn't get a helicopter, but we didn't need one; our words to each other were exciting enough. We'd purposefully held off saying those three special ones, though I think we both knew we felt them. We wanted to give each other the grand finale we deserved. We wanted to tie the bow together. Glenn spoke first. He stood in front of me and listed what he loved about us as a couple and what he loved about me. The producers had made us practise our speeches beforehand but Glenn went off-script and spoke for about a minute longer than mandated.

I spoke next, beginning by telling him he was unlike any other man I'd met.

'You are fiercely loyal, you are kind and you are compassionate. You have made me feel valued, appreciated and loved like I have never experienced with a partner before. You have shifted my world, you have made me completely re-evaluate how I think about love and relationships. You have shown me a deeper love.'

And then we said, 'I love you.' Our big finish.

Instead of giving each other roses, we both reached for rings. As it turned out, we did get to choose them ourselves. Marti had sat with me under a pagoda and had presented a collection of four. Glenn and I fumbled and laughed as we tried to put them on each other. In our last interview, I announced I had a hot boyfriend and we told each other we loved each other again. The credits rolled at half-screen, just under Glenn twirling me, silhouetted by the Fijian sunset. My voice narrated the scene for a final time.

'I am so glad I came to *Paradise*, I'm so glad I took a chance again on this experience, because look what I've found. Glenn is perfect and I've been a little bit worried about perfect, but in this moment, at this commitment ceremony . . . yeah, it is perfect and I'm just embracing all the perfect.'

CHAPTER 9

Perfect

Glenn and I negotiated with the producers to have a weekend in Sydney together after the show. Glenn's flight to Perth had to go through Sydney anyway so we asked if we could push back the connecting flight until Monday. They agreed on the proviso we flew separately and Glenn was discreet as he travelled to my house in Summer Hill.

It was a sharp shift from the artificial world of the show: from fairy lights, filming and constant monitoring to sitting in my living room entirely alone. The feeling was both freeing and exposing, with no one telling us when to eat, drink or kiss. Osher wasn't going to walk into the kitchen to kick off a rose ceremony in which Glenn would affirm his love for me. Gone were the meetings planned by production to introduce us to each other's closest friends and family. Gone were the intricate dates to progress the relationship. We had to do it all ourselves.

In those first moments, we savoured the simple things. We took our first selfie as we lay in my bed together and we scrolled through each other's Instagram and Facebook feeds, showing each other our lives as we presented them to the world. I showed Glenn a picture of me with Shannon Noll from four or five years ago, when as president of the Student Union I'd managed to get him to play at our uni's orientation week. It remained one of my proudest achievements.

Glenn showed me a Facebook album of blurry pictures from EDM festival *Tomorrowland*. They were from 2013. I leant over him, clicking on one that stood out from the rest: he had a buzz cut and was wearing a long, ripped, white singlet that read in big serif text IBIZA HOUSE FUCKIN' MAFIA. I snorted. That twenty-four-year-old boy was such a leap away from the composed, calm man lying in bed with me, the one I'd met four weeks ago.

With our phones glowing above us, I learnt that Glenn had been to every single night of The Living End's six-show retrospective tour in Perth and I told him about how I used to finish every night clubbing with a meat pie from 7-Eleven. In a way, it felt like we were meeting each other again for the first time, now that we were able to see each other's moments and memories. We lay on my bed for hours, looking through our lives together.

In the morning, we walked around the corner to get coffee. We got a buzz out of flouting the rules a little, which prohibited us from being in public together, though realistically no one was going to recognise either of us. In the afternoon, we took an Uber to see Glenn's sister, Lisa, who lived in Bondi.

There was no narrative, no producers pushing for 'jeopardy', just a guy introducing a girl to his sister. We sat around with coffees and unpacked the last month. We told her about our initial magnetism, joked about Glenn's mum watching our R-rated dates and laughed as I relayed my one-on-one time with Neil to her.

Producers had set Neil and I up for our chat on the beach, but in order for the camera crew to get clear shots of our heads as we spoke, they'd had us stand five metres apart. I'd basically had to shout at him; a very natural way to get to know your potential boyfriend's brother.

When we got home from Bondi, we watched the movie *Hot Rod*, with what would become our regular Thai order sitting on our knees: green chicken curry, beef pad kee mao, and golden bags at Glenn's request. We imitated Andy Samberg's 'wh' in 'wwwwhiskey', swapping quotes from the movie as it played out on screen.

Before he left, I'd also made sure to introduce him to Bobette, showing him the pages and pages of commentary on the forums about his season of *The Bachelorette*. He was as captivated by the detail as I'd been when I'd first discovered them and laughed to learn that his original moniker had been 'Metallic Jacket' because of his outfit of choice on the red carpet. I could see a little smile break across his face as he read that a user called 'Sundy' said they really liked him and an even bigger one when he'd seen Bobette's reply. 'So wholesome,' they'd said.

Glenn flew back to Perth on Monday morning and I took the train into work. It had not improved. A new general secretary had started in the role but the office was no more unified or comfortable. His time was spent cleaning up the mess that ICAC had left and placating union bosses. Most of the staff were counting down the days until NSW Labor would close for the Christmas break.

I limped through the first week, the comedown from shooting aggravated by just how demoralising the office environment was. Throughout the days, I messaged Glenn, sharing little windows into my life in an attempt to stay connected. It felt stilted compared to our time together. He sent me a selfie with his work ute parked outside a Dome. I scrolled through my camera roll to send a picture back, picking between twenty different iterations of the same lift selfie that I'd clearly been determined to get just right.

We'd already had pretty extensive conversations in *Paradise* about how it would all work once we were back in the 'real world' and continued those conversations while Glenn was in Sydney. We agreed that long distance was not ideal but it was how things were going to have to be for a while: Glenn had a burgeoning business in Perth and we both felt that after four weeks it was too soon to be contemplating any permanent moves. We agreed to some loose principles of trying to see each other once a month, at minimum. He would fly to Sydney and I would fly to Perth. It would be expensive, but it would be temporary.

Before he'd left, we'd sat down with our calendars. It was the end of November and we decided to map out the next few months, assuming that *Bachelor in Paradise* would air around April. We started with a trip to Sydney. Jackson Garlick was throwing a birthday pub crawl in a fortnight and had invited most of the cast. Attending would be very naughty but most of the cast judged our contracts to be malleable, to say the least. We decided that if multiple cast members were in attendance, and we resolved to keep our hands off each other, we'd be fine to attend. Glenn booked flights. That trip would cover off December and we planned to reunite in Darwin just after Christmas. We were set through to the New Year.

In addition to our texts throughout the workday, we FaceTimed at night. I'd relay the monotony of my workday and he'd tell me things about air conditioning that I didn't understand. I'd update him on any goss I'd found on the forums recently and we traded weekend plans.

I was having a quiet one. For the past few days at work, I'd felt my body give me a signal just past midday: it wanted a G&T. We'd drunk so much and so consistently in Fiji that I was actually having withdrawals. It felt awful so I'd decided it was time for a detox. Big walks each day, nourishing food at every meal, maybe one glass of wine on the weekend.

Glenn was going to his mate's thirtieth. It was Hawaiian themed. He balanced his phone against a water bottle on his side table and clambered over the bed to his wardrobe, pulling out a party shirt covered with palm trees and flamingos.

'What do you think?' he asked me.

'It's perfect.'

I'd never wanted to be the type to live for the weekend, or for my mood to be dictated by what day it was. But with work the way it was, once Friday rolled around, I nearly updated my Facebook status to TGIF.

I had planned a relaxed dinner to catch up with Hannah and on Friday night and went to a Christmas party for an organisation I volunteered with called Gig Buddies on Saturday. Glenn sent me a selfie of him in his flamingo shirt with his friends. I sent back a photo of my friend Myra tearing up the dancefloor at the Chrissy party. I was in bed by nine p.m.

I woke on Sunday morning the freshest and most clear-headed I'd felt in a while. I felt pride in my lack of hangover and leant into a full morning cosplaying as 'that girl'.

The girl that wakes at five a.m. and meditates on a yoga mat facing the sun. The girl that makes her bed, lights some incense and journals for half an hour. That girl is thriving. She's got her shit together. All areas of her life are handled. Love? Tick. Fitness? Tick. Family? Tick.

I grabbed a string shopping bag from the very back of my underwear drawer that I'd bought from Kmart a year ago thinking I'd use it every weekend and left the house to grab some fresh bread and vegetables. I decided I'd go check out our local markets for the first time. I don't think I'd ever been awake early enough on a Sunday before to make that happen. On the way, I rang Mum to debrief about Fiji more fully and even sent my dad a text without any specific agenda, just checking in. When I got to the markets, I bought a big green juice and a wax candle with the intention of finding a guided meditation on YouTube when I got home.

I felt like I'd been striving to be 'that girl' all my life. It had started small. In high school, I'd always felt proud if I had all my shit together at the same time. Then, it meant having an organised wallet, relatively clean schoolbag and phone without a cracked screen. Now, it meant paying for a gym membership I rarely used, and trying to make lentil dhal. It meant implementing a skincare routine, finding out what tretinoin does and washing my clothes on the right setting. I was never very good at it. The one time I did try to make dhal, I'd put in one-eighth of a tablespoon of cinnamon, instead of one-eighth of a teaspoon. I didn't want to admit my failure, so took cinnamon dhal to work for the entire week.

I was halfway through looking up what setting I should use for linen when Glenn called me on FaceTime. He looked rough: his eyes were tired and his naked chest was visible at the bottom of the screen. He was the antithesis of 'that girl', very much still in bed.

'Big night?' I greeted him.

He nodded. He told me he just needed the comfort of a quick chat and then he was going to take some Panadol and go back to sleep. I joked that I thought he was match fit, basking in my lack of hangover once more. I told him I would be manifesting his return to health and balanced the phone on the dryer as I loaded the washing machine.

I decided to round off my ultra-productive day with a trip to Broadway Shopping Centre in Glebe to get an early start on Christmas presents—or, at least, earlier than I had ever managed before. I purchased a range of very thoughtful gifts for each family member, including a disposable camera for Glenn, intended to help us catalogue our future memories, then I grabbed some takeaway sashimi to complete the wholesomeness.

Glenn surfaced a couple of hours after I'd finished dinner, just as I was preparing to brush my teeth and go to bed.

He messaged. *'Can I ring?'*

As soon as I received it, I felt something was off. Of course he could ring. There had never been any formality any other time we'd called each other.

'Of course, babe,' I replied. Almost as soon as I sent it, he was FaceTiming me. I walked into my bedroom and sat on my bed, getting comfortable against the pillows before sliding my finger against the screen to accept.

'Is Hannah around?' he asked. It was a weird question.

'She is,' I said, 'but I'm in my room.'

He began. 'Alisha, I have to tell you about something that happened last night.' His face looked different than it had during our cursory call earlier this morning. He didn't just look hungover, he looked pale and serious. 'I kissed Helena last night.' His face fell. My heart fell.

Helena? Kissed? I had to take a moment to place her in my mind. Helena from the show. The Helena he'd been hanging out with but nothing had progressed. I was silent for a moment. My mind whirred, trying to put together the pieces. His selfie in his flamingo shirt, his mate's thirtieth.

'What the fuck,' I said aloud, directly into the camera.

Glenn looked solemn. He looked hurt, a mirror of my pain, which I resented. He started crying. I wanted to comfort him and I hated that. But then my thoughts ran out of my mouth in a hurry. I was sounding angrier than I expected.

'Are you fucking serious?' I asked, as tears rolled down his cheeks. 'You are fucking kidding me.' Each sentence was punctuated by profanities. I was grasping for them desperately to somehow express my pain.

'I was not meant to be this person this year.'

'I was not meant to be the heartbroken one.'

'That was last year. This was meant to be different.'

I was speaking to him cruelly. My voice didn't match the hurt in my heart—it was like I'd somehow been split in two, with someone stronger and meaner defending the hurt part of me. The mean person took over.

'You've ruined everything,' I told him. 'You've ruined us. What could have been. Our future.'

'You have ruined this,' I repeated, feeling hot tears start to well in my eyes. When I felt the tears, I became even more single-minded. This conversation was over.

'I am getting off the phone,' I told him. 'I am ringing Alex.'

I hung up, fucking furious. My face was red and hot and I sat still on the bed for a moment, gathering my thoughts. Before I called Alex, I walked outside to our balcony, where Hannah was sitting on our wooden outdoor setting. I stood in the doorway, propping the weight of it open with one arm.

'You won't fucking believe what happened,' I told her, like I was about to launch into some juicy gossip. 'Glenn cheated on me.'

I told her, with an almost surprised-sounding upward inflection, what he had done.

I didn't stay in the doorway to unpack it with her for long. I told her what I had told Glenn. 'I am ringing Alex.'

She nodded. Her love and presence were all the solidarity that I needed. I walked back into my bedroom and rang Alex, without a thought to it being after eight-thirty on a Sunday night. I took a breath as the phone rang and stared at my bed, which I'd spent the day lovingly assembling with fresh sheets and a new throw.

I felt like I was out of my own body. I was acting out a drama that wasn't my real life. I was on one of those old shows that played before the six p.m. news. *Days of our Lives* or *The Bold and the Beautiful*. It almost felt comical. I should have been dramatically delivering news to someone with their back turned to me. Alex answered and I launched in, introducing the matter with the new cadence that had taken over—like I was telling a story about someone I didn't know.

'Alex, you won't believe what has happened,' I said. Then I told her what he had told me. He had been out for a friend's birthday. Helena had seen he was out and had messaged him to come to a house party. He had gone to the party and at one point during the evening they had kissed.

'He was extremely drunk,' I heard myself offer in justification.

Alex was equally shocked. This wasn't like Glenn; or at least, it wasn't what was expected of Glenn. He was meant to be an upstanding guy, the loyal guy, the guy you wanted to marry. Glenn had been presented as the antithesis to your reality TV fuckboy. He was meant to be trustworthy.

Alex comforted me, as she'd done countless times before. 'It's going to be okay.'

There were messages from Glenn waiting for me when I hung up.

'I don't want to lose you. This is truly out of character for me.'

I replied immediately, cuttingly. *Just glad I didn't waste my time for the next four months.'*

I felt like I'd been royally ripped off. I'd allowed myself to get excited about a future that had been just as quickly taken away. I opened a bottle of wine and Hannah sat with me on our balcony until we'd finished it. I just kept repeating that I couldn't believe it. She encouraged me to upload a thirst trap, which I did and then deleted. I eventually tried to put myself to bed, scared I wouldn't be able to escape my thoughts, but whether it was the wine, or the emotional whiplash, sleep came.

I didn't speak to Glenn the next day or the day after that. I'd read somewhere on Reddit that one of the most important things that must happen after the cheatee discovers the cheating is to allow the emotional reaction to occur before even attempting to make rational decisions. As I was predisposed to acting impulsively, the idea had stayed with me.

I wasn't completely falling apart, which was gratifying: what Glenn had done had seemingly not destroyed my entire sense of self. While I was deeply hurt and unsure of my next step, my self-talk remained, for the most part, balanced. It seemed like progress.

But I still felt out of control and I wanted to control something. Something in my life had to change. I wasn't delusional about happiness—I knew it ebbed and flowed—but the stark return to life as normal had shown me in a matter of weeks that I wasn't happy. The melancholy was deep in my core and had gotten comfortable.

At work, my colleague Jess came into my office to discuss something inconsequential. Jess and I had become each other's rocks in the office. We'd discuss how awful we were both feeling in the office or vent about some ridiculous mess she was having to clean up: dealing with a member who didn't understand why they weren't Party president, or a branch that had fallen apart.

Jess had barely sat down when I started to sob uncontrollably. It was the first time I'd properly cried since Glenn had told me on Sunday night. I couldn't tell her about the cheating, she didn't even know I'd met someone. Besides, I couldn't even be sure that that was why my body was reacting in this way. I think I just felt sorry for myself in general.

I leant on the work stuff to explain away my tears: how sorry I felt for Kaila. How isolated I felt in the office. How little respect I felt some of the senior members of staff had for me.

Jess had always been solutions-focused and after seeing me start crying, seemingly out of nowhere, she was no different.

She spoke calmly and with consideration. 'I think you should type out a resignation letter and just look at it and see how you feel.'

There was something in the finality of her suggestion that made me feel better immediately. She sat with me as I typed it out and by the time I had typed, 'Please let me know how I can help through the transition period,' I wasn't crying anymore. I was excited.

Jess had been proofreading over my shoulder as I typed it out. 'Looks good,' she said. 'Now just save it in your drafts while you mull it over.'

I wasn't going to mull it over. It felt right. I moved my cursor up to the 'Send' button and pressed it dramatically, looking over my shoulder at Jess for shock value. She did look shocked but also a little bit nervous. Maybe I was having a full-on breakdown and her course of action had been a mistake? She was right though. With the email out of my inbox and into the ether, I felt better than I had in a long time. I quickly assured her that I was okay. I had money coming from Warner Brothers and this was a fresh start. It was okay. I was okay.

Jess gave me a hug and went back to her desk. I sat alone with my phone.

'*I quit my job,*' I messaged Glenn.

Despite the fact that we hadn't spoken for two days, he responded instantly with congratulations. He told me he was proud of me. He knew how deeply unhappy I had been. Another text bubble appeared after a few minutes.

'Can we talk?' he asked.

I agreed and said I'd call him on the way home from work. I decided to get off the train at the stop before mine. It was a fifteen-minute walk that I could extend to twenty by dawdling. I was comforted walking through the familiar Inner West streets, lined with similar terrace houses. *I have done hard things before and I can do them again*, I told myself as I walked. I dialled Glenn's number.

The conversation opened with his apologies, the same as on Sunday night. His voice wobbled slightly, attempting to moderate his tone. It sounded like he'd had a rough couple of days. He told me that he'd spent half an hour crying outside a Subway after picking up his lunch. I was trying my best to stay serious and stony-faced but I couldn't help but let out a laugh, imagining him sitting in his Ford Ranger bawling over a chipotle chicken wrap. I stifled my laugh with my free hand, realising I probably sounded insensitive.

'Sorry,' I blurted. 'Oh, I'm so sorry. This is really hard, I know, I am really, really sorry that you are having a hard time.'

I meant it. He was genuine; I could tell from the tremor in his voice and the specificity of his story, and I was empathetic. I'd been in his position before. I'd cheated, I'd caused someone immense pain and as difficult as it can be to concede when you are on the receiving end of the betrayal, I knew Glenn was in pain as well.

'I've been talking to Alex,' he said.

'That's good, I'm really glad,' I responded. He told me Alex had advised him to let me contact him first. I thanked him and told him I had appreciated the space.

As the conversation moved into harder territory, my tone became serious. I told him that if there was any chance of us getting through this, I needed to know every detail of what had happened. I didn't want to know, but I felt if there was any chance of us moving forward it was necessary. I needed to know the truth. *Was it just a kiss? Did they fuck? Why did they kiss?* The questions all sat on the tip of my tongue.

Glenn started to unpack the night in more detail than our five-minute FaceTime on Sunday, leading with the emphatic assertion that it was just a kiss. He told me again that he'd had way too much to drink and that she'd messaged him to come to a house party. He told me he'd been excited to reunite with a castmate, and I half bought it. I knew the feeling of wanting to be around the people you'd just shared such an intense experience with again. But I didn't generally hook up with them. He told me they'd ended up chatting on a tennis court in the backyard and that's where it had happened.

He said it had been short and meaningless. I didn't buy that. It must have had meaning.

As he recounted the night, my resentment started to rise, and as soon as he'd finished I launched into the next order of business. Glenn had a flight booked to Sydney on Friday, two days from now. I was meant to be picking him up from the airport. We were meant to be going to Jackson Garlick's birthday together.

My word choice was extremely melodramatic. 'You've forfeited your right to come to Garlo's,' I said. My syntax matched my emotion but I was also talking about a golf-themed pub crawl so my invocation of rights was maybe a little much. It felt good though, like I was reclaiming some control. Most of our *Paradise* cast would be celebrating together on Saturday, and I wanted to be there with them.

Glenn agreed but said he still wanted to talk to me in person. He still wanted to come to Sydney. He was happy to change his flight so we could speak on the Sunday and he would return that same night. I thought that that was reasonable—even admirable that he'd go to that effort to sit down with me in person.

With the immediate plans squared away, I moved on to my next agenda item. It was something that had been eating away at me for the past two days: embarrassment. Specifically, I felt embarrassed about having to tell Mum what had happened. After all the theatrics of *Paradise*, after the now eerie lines about Glenn and I being too good to be true, I was going to have to tell her that they'd been right, it *had* been too good to be true. She would feel my pain again, a pain she'd seen envelop me after my first season of *Bachelor in Paradise*.

I asked him to tell her. I told him that I was dreading it and that him telling her would go some way to getting us back on track, even though I was unsure if that was even something I wanted yet. I thought it was a bold ask, something I'd never be prepared to do but Glenn agreed without hesitation and called her the very next day. She approached it like she approached everything, with empathy, which only served to confuse me more. I was knee-deep in Facebook groups and forums filled with women who at the slightest mention of cheating would urge the poster to dump them. It was something I'd ordinarily respond with too. Decisive and determined. It felt wrong to be even considering entertaining our relationship again.

On Saturday, I went to Garlo's alone. I dug up an old polyester shirt I'd worn playing lawn bowls at uni, and paired it with a short white skirt, knee-high white socks and white tennis shoes.

I took the extra time to attach some false eyelashes, intending to flood my Instagram with stories and selfies meant solely for Glenn. A bunch of the cast were already at the party when I arrived: Jamie, Britt, Ciarran and Kiki, plus a guy called Scot who'd come in late in the season.

I was so happy to be back with everybody and we went hard at the first couple of pubs, sculling drinks and throwing back too many shots of Fireball. By early afternoon, our cohort was far from sober, and the more I drank the closer to the surface recent developments came. I held it together for a good three hours, but when we arrived at The Lord Dudley and one of my castmates congratulated me on Glenn and I making it to the end, I burst into tears. I told them what had happened. I told them all what had happened. Nobody could believe it. I started to drink more, to dull the anxiety of knowing the secret was out and I had been the one to leak it.

By the time we got to the last bar, The Imperial in Paddington, I was not in a good way. I could hardly keep my balance and was ready to talk about Glenn to anybody who would listen. My target was Scot, who had been on his season of *The Bachelorette* as well as with us on *Bachelor in Paradise*.

We found ourselves sitting in the gutter between parked cars. While I started talking about Glenn, at some point it sharply pivoted to me compelling Scot to come back to my house. It had only just passed eight p.m. but at my urging, Scot relented and we got into a twenty-minute Uber to my place in Summer Hill.

Hannah was still awake and ran into us in the living room as I hightailed it to my room, bumping into our Kmart ottoman on the way. Hannah and I never interfered in each other's chaos, so she said a polite hello and told us she was going out to the balcony for a smoke. I closed my bedroom door behind us.

Nothing about sleeping with Scot was romantic or considered. I was a mess and my room was a mess. I practically fell onto the bed, it happened and then it was over. It took just long enough to register as a reality, and a mistake. I had been lying on the mattress for little more than a moment when dread crept across my whole body—I wanted to be anywhere but that bed. I looked at Scot, who was also staring up at the ceiling.

'Can we go back to the party?' I said.

He was obliging and we left while Hannah was still finishing her cigarette on the balcony.

In the Uber, travelling back across the suburbs of Sydney with Scot in tow, I decided to message Glenn.

'What time do you land?' I typed.

He replied straightaway. *'I already have. I'm checking into my hotel in Surry Hills.'*

The fogginess of multiple shots and too many pints immediately parted and I felt alert for the first time in hours. Before I even knew what I was doing, I turned to Scot and said, 'I think I'm going to go see Glenn.'

Scot really didn't care. I didn't need to explain to him that Glenn had landed, or that he was currently a handful of suburbs away, or that I'd already messaged him for the hotel name. He was fine with it. I added a stop to our trip, and when we pulled up Scot wished me luck and continued back to Garlo's party. I was grateful to him for being so cool about it. I was officially back in battering-ram mode, something I'd worked really hard to try to escape, but I didn't know how else to be. I was just leaping from one emotion to the next and as I travelled up the lift to Glenn's level, the next was anger.

Glenn opened his hotel door to a scene. He was completely sober. I was trashed. I stumbled into his room and now that we were together, in person, I called him a range of names before hugging myself into his chest. He helped me to the bed and I started to cry, provoked by the teeny act of kindness. It was the most I'd cried all week. I told him what I'd just done with Scot, apologising through tears. It had been completely out of spite, such an ugly emotion. Glenn had hurt me and I had wanted to hurt him. I'd wanted to get even. I sat on the bed in a ball, oscillating between shame, regret and hurt. Eventually, I began to calm down. I lay on my side and Glenn held me. I put my face under his chin to try to mask how much I smelled like alcohol and he rubbed my back with one hand, trying to help slow my breathing. We lay on the bed for hours. Him in his clothes from the flight, me in the polyester polo and white skirt that I'd put back on to try to erase the last four hours and hide anything that had happened. I didn't know it then, but once I fell asleep, Glenn left to walk the empty streets of Surry Hills alone. He walked aimlessly through the unfamiliar city, up one street, down another and then around the block. No doubt making his own judgements about what I had just done.

I woke with the same throb in my head as the first time Glenn and I had shared a bed. His arm was draped heavily across me, hugging my stomach. When I rolled over, the first words out of my mouth were an apology.

'I'm so sorry,' I told him. Now, I seemed to understand the concept of short and meaningless. The only real motivation behind what had happened last night was to attain some sort of messed-up reciprocal justice. I hated that at the first sign of pressure, my instinct had been to even the score. But it hadn't worked: I didn't particularly feel better about what Glenn had done to me, I had just dished out more hurt. I could feel myself excusing my own behaviour, where I had cast Glenn as the sum total of his transgression. I could feel the binaries of bad and good slipping away; I was no longer the angel I'd held myself up to be, and Glenn perhaps wasn't the devil my Facebook groups were telling me.

Relationship therapist Esther Perel says that catastrophe has a way of propelling us into the essence of things and that is what it did for Glenn and me. If the fairy lights and lanterns of *Bachelor in Paradise* were artifice to propel us towards love, then Glenn's kiss with Helena and my vengeful reaction had ripped us right back into reality.

Our superficial chats in the weeks after Fiji would have been sufficient to maintain a relationship until we happily announced that we were still together on *The Project* or *Studio 10* in four months' time. But I'm not sure they would have resulted in us really understanding each other, or led to a deep long-term partnership.

But now, conversations about work and weekends were suddenly replaced with broad philosophical conversations about love, relationships, monogamy and boundaries. Topics we often think we've unpacked with our partners when we've really only scratched the surface.

We left Glenn's hotel at his check-out time and took an Uber to the markets I had been to exactly one week before. We bought coffees from a van and sat down in the nearby park dotted with people going about their Sunday. Noisy kids clambered over colourful metal play equipment, their parents watching on.

In that beautiful tableau of a Sydney weekend, Glenn and I sat and talked. We talked about what we thought about love, what it really meant to us and why we felt compelled to find a partner. We talked about monogamy and the romantic ruse that if you were truly in love you were expected to never be attracted to another person again, which didn't seem realistic to either of us. We faced what happens when you meet someone else that gives you that dopamine rush. We volleyed back and forth, setting boundaries. What's worse: an ongoing flirtation or a physical transgression? We didn't always have concrete answers, but we were enjoying diving into the questions all the same.

It might be difficult to comprehend, but ultimately I became grateful for that time. Everything that I came to value most about Glenn was on display as we sat in that park drinking our cooling coffees. We had considerably disappointed each other, and with that disappointment the layers of performance had to be shed. We were seeing each other for exactly who we were. Our conversations weren't about Helena and they weren't about Scot. They were about us and where we were going next.

In Esther Perel's work, she identifies three basic post-infidelity outcomes for couples that choose to stay together. Those who cannot escape the past, where the betrayal becomes a black hole that ensnares both parties in an endless round of bitterness, revenge and blame. She calls them sufferers. Those who choose to move past the infidelity, not necessarily transcending it, but trying, she calls the builders. For some, the betrayal is transformative. These couples come to see the infidelity as an event that, though insanely painful, contained the seeds of something positive. She calls them the explorers. We liked that one. We decided we were committed explorers.

By the end of the weekend, we'd made a mutual commitment to forgiveness. We had decided to give our relationship another chance. We wouldn't be back where we were overnight, but hopefully we could end up in an even better place.

Our crisis let us explore each other's hearts in a way that we might never otherwise have done. Sometimes, I fear that without it we would have stayed in the paradisiacal fantasy of fairy lights and perfection. It was beautiful, but it wasn't real. It was a fairytale.

CHAPTER 10

Happily Ever After

The next time Glenn and I saw each other, in person, was just after Christmas for our trip to Darwin. We stayed with a group of mutual friends we'd collected from the show. Everything that had happened was still raw but the trip was exactly what we needed to continue to rebuild. Everyone we were with knew what had happened and they understood that we had decided to stay together. None of them moralised or tried to offer up their opinion. They just treated us with compassion and care, trusting that we had made our decision for a reason. After a week of jaunting through the Top End and having a particularly rowdy night at Throb, Darwin's premiere LGBTQI+ nightclub, we had plans to drive down to Kakadu, just us two. We picked up a hire car and drove through Jabiru, stopping for the best salad sandwich of our lives and then hiked through Ubirr, until we were high above the Nadab floodplain. The long drives between Darwin and Kakadu served as the perfect venue to continue to delve deeper, reconstructing the foundations of our relationship. We covered everything: our obscure family histories, what we were like as kids, our greatest fears and our hopes for the future.

We introduced our friends like characters in a play. Glenn would give me all the contextual details about someone who was important to him—how they met, where they lived, what they did—before shifting into a more sensitive register, describing how their relationship was evolving as they grew older. How he wished they were as close as they used to be.

I told him about the Labor Party, about Kaila. I told him how distressing it had been to see someone so quickly cast aside, to see their former friends and confidants rip them apart, as if that's what the public demanded. He told me about starting his business and about living in Perth, selling it to me like he was being paid by Tourism Western Australia themselves.

In Kakadu, we mapped out our movements for the next months ahead. I hadn't travelled much in my twenties; I'd been too busy canvassing the voters of Western Sydney. So having left my job with the Party, I decided I owed myself a little bit of a trip. Perth turned out to be an excellent stopover from Southeast Asia so I structured my travels around our visits. First, I'd head to Bali for a month, and Glenn would come over in the middle. He'd visit for four nights just in time for Valentine's Day. Then I'd come back to Perth for a few days, before heading to Cambodia for just over a fortnight. My adventures would lead me right up until the end of March, which was perfect, given we were expecting the show to air in April.

After Darwin, Glenn and I fell into a relaxed rhythm. On my first trip to Perth, he delivered on his promise to take me to Gnomesville: driving us down south with a pair of gnomes from Bunnings riding on the dash. We named them Sherman and Poppy and once we arrived at the seemingly million-strong throng of gnomes, we placed them in a corner filled with friendly faces.

When he came over to Bali, we bounced around beach clubs without a second thought about the fact that we were technically meant to be in 'hiding'. And when I returned to Perth, he showed me all his favourite places: his favourite beach, his favourite place to get coffee and his favourite weekend getaways. I documented the memories fastidiously, organising the pictures and videos I took into a folder labelled 'Paradise'. I was already bursting with ideas for how I would one day present our relationship to the world.

Though everything was tracking well, we weren't without our moments. The kiss with Helena had left some lingering insecurities, which popped up unhelpfully. Like on our road trip with Poppy and Sherman, where I'd been having a stalk of Glenn's Instagram feed as he popped into a petrol station to pay for our fuel. I was scrolling through years of travel with his ex-girlfriend and stopped on a picture he'd posted of them positioned against a lush island backdrop. He was giving her a piggyback and they were both smiling into the camera, framed by a palm tree. 'Enjoying the island life!' he'd captioned the photo, adding the hashtags #islandlife and #littlecorn. I felt a twang of jealousy. We were having fun together but I longed to get to that comfortable state where you have years of shared history, cute nicknames and inside jokes. We were still at the stage where you weren't sure if it was okay if you reached over and ate a bit of the other person's food. Where you'd tell an off-colour joke and you'd fear they'd think you were a terrible person. Where you'd feel as though you needed to transfer them $6.50 if they shouted you a beer.

When Glenn returned to the car and we were a couple of minutes down the road, I brought up his South American travels. 'Everywhere you went looked so beautiful,' I said slowly. 'And your nickname for your ex was so cute.'

'What nickname?' he asked.

'Little corn,' I responded.

He laughed. 'What are you on about?'

'In your picture, in Nicaragua, you called her little corn.'

'Babe, Little Corn is the island we were staying on.'

My face flushed red, and I laughed at myself and he laughed at me. Only I could spin a simple geographical hashtag into an established part of their romantic relationship.

I was just finishing my Cambodia trip in late March when the world began to change. Covid-19 was growing increasingly serious and I arrived back in Sydney just as the government began to introduce the first social-distancing measures and isolation requirements. Living rooms around the country adapted to a new daily rhythm of press conferences and we all spoke a new language of contact tracing and quarantine. Now, slumped on our couch waiting for the NSW premier's eleven a.m. briefing, our Bintangs in Bali seemed like a mirage.

Each day brought higher case numbers and new announcements: stimulus packages, stock-market crashes and, eventually, border closures. Glenn and I were in constant contact, sending each other articles and tweets tracking the unfolding situation, but it wasn't until I received a text from a friend who worked for the McGowan Government, whom I'd enthusiastically told I was dating a Western Australian, that we started to have serious conversations about what these lockdowns and travel restrictions might mean for us.

'*Apparently McGowan wants to block all non-freight travel,*' my friend's message said. I took a screenshot and forwarded it to Glenn. By now, we'd been officially dating for just on four months and the idea of being separated for a long time didn't appeal to either of us.

I had little keeping me in Sydney now that I'd left my job, and I'd come to see the city as increasingly suffocating. Everyone seemed to have their eyes on what everyone else was doing. Where they were working and what they were working towards. How much they were likely paid and how it compared to everyone else. Everything felt hyper-competitive, whether it was work, money or your future. Unemployed and waiting for the show to air, I felt the city constricting around me. Trialling Perth for a few months didn't seem like a bad idea. By the end of a fifteen-minute FaceTime discussing the prospect with Glenn, I'd bought a one-way ticket.

Glenn was in the process of moving into a new place amid the Covid-19 chaos. He'd been planning to live with Neil and now they'd have a third wheel. Neil, who was then a camera operator at Channel 7, was on assignment covering the crisis in London, so when we picked up the house keys and headed over, it was just Glenn and me. It was a three-bedroom home with a big backyard in a suburb called Como, fifteen minutes from the CBD. During our first week together, we ate pizza on the living room floor so many times it lost any charm. Glenn's parents thankfully brought us over boxes of hand-me-down crockery and cooking essentials and we managed to assemble a neat little kitchen with the few things that we had.

Though we both jumped to reunite in the chaos, we still hadn't explicitly discussed our future plans. I'd come armed with two suitcases full of clothes and I was still paying rent in Sydney for another four months, until my lease with Hannah ended. Glenn told me he was more than happy to cover the cost of the Perth place for us both, but I didn't want him to think I was making myself too comfortable so as he unboxed and hung his clothes onto new sets of coat hangers, I shoved a handful of T-shirts and a few pairs of jeans into one little cubby in the corner of the wardrobe. I left the rest of my clothes in my suitcases in the spare room, trying to be as little of an imposition as possible.

We were only a week into playing house when we learnt that the airing of the show was going to be delayed. Renee sent me a link to a *Daily Mail* article: 'Channel Ten confirms *Bachelor in Paradise* is postponed due to the coronavirus pandemic—with the network airing Jamie Oliver specials instead.' A spokesperson from the network was quoted in the article telling fans not to panic, the series would air in the coming months. I immediately checked the forums, which had been quiet for months. They couldn't understand why it had been shelved either.

'It must be so frustrating as a contestant this season to keep the "ending" a secret so much longer than planned,' someone commented.

'Sounds to me like they're planning to air it in late July or August when *The Bachelor* would usually air,' Bobette replied. Bobette would turn out to be correct. We'd have to wait until August for the show to begin.

With *Bachelor in Paradise* pushed back and borders looking unlikely to reopen anytime soon, I settled into life in Perth. It wasn't totally unfamiliar. I had a handful of friends on the west coast from dating Tom and my days in student politics. Tom had been a Labor guy, so my knowledge of Perth principally featured a primary school in Armadale, where we'd first made out while manning an election booth during a by-election; Crown Towers, where we'd crashed The University of Western Australia's Law Ball; and Sizzler Innaloo.

I attempted to expand my geographical range by pointing at places mentioned on the six p.m. news and asking Glenn to explain where they were in relation to us. I attempted to expand my network by reconnecting with people from student politics and Glenn began to slowly introduce me to the people in his life. Neil and his now boyfriend of six months, Marty, also moved into the Como house. We introduced Glenn to *RuPaul's Drag Race* and finally redecorated now that we had a critical mass of stuff.

Perth's evolution into my permanent home was in many ways more practical than romantic. McGowan wasn't letting me out anytime soon and I needed money. I needed a job.

For the first time, Warner Brothers had separated our payments for the show. Instead of receiving one lump sum, we were to receive half when we finished shooting and the other half when the show finished airing. It was intended to incentivise the cast not to leak spoilers or the results of the show. It was introduced when a finale couple from season two—Alex Nation and Bill Goldsmith—set up pap pics of them making out in a Melbourne dog park just days after we'd finished shooting.

The new pay structure meant I had been subsisting on my meagre savings and now Centrelink payments. I started to seriously apply for work, sending off dozens of applications each week, but with Covid-19 gripping the country it was hard to know whether employers were serious about hiring. After a month of applications, I'd received no replies. No interviews, no polite rejections: radio silence. I started to fear it wasn't Covid but my involvement with the show.

I reached out to an old contact for advice. Lenda knew the Perth business and political landscape like the back of her hand. She had a similar vibe to Kaila: she emanated power, supported young women and took no prisoners. She'd recently left a position at WA Labor, where she'd been the assistant secretary through McGowan's first election. Now, she was running the west coast arm of a lobbying outfit. I sent her my CV and cover letter. I didn't know how to mention *The Bachelor*, or whether I should mention it at all. It just felt so awkward.

'I thrive in high pressure environments and have excellent oral communication skills, as demonstrated by my time on *The Bachelor* and *Bachelor in Paradise*.'

I didn't want to include it, but I figured that prospective employers had Google and if they searched my name, they might feel I was deliberately omitting a big aspect of my life. I hoped Lenda would know what to do. I also dared to hope that she might take pity on me and keep me in her thoughts when some exec at a business breakfast mentioned they were looking for a new employee.

Lenda did one better: she offered me a month of contract work at her lobbying outfit. Lobbying was a common step on the political staffing pipeline. You joined Young Labor, worked in an electorate office, were promoted into a shadow minister or minister's office, depending on the colour of the current government, and once you were sick of that you took your skills and connections to various lobbying firms around Australia. It seemed like a natural fit and I couldn't be more grateful for the pay cheque. At the end of the contract, Lenda offered me a role as a consultant.

By this point, *Bachelor in Paradise* was about to premiere and I wanted her to be fully informed about what the next eight weeks of airing would look like. The afternoon she gave me the formal job offer, I leant against a desk in her office that faced onto Perth's CBD and fumbled my talking points, eventually getting out that the show was about to air.

'It'll run for a couple of weeks,' I said. I added that I might have to do a couple of media interviews here and there and there might be a couple of things published in the paper.

Lenda, like Kaila, couldn't care less. She responded with a blunt, 'Do you do anything fucked?'

'Not really,' I replied slowly.

'Then I don't care.' She couldn't have said four better words. I felt so indebted to her and started to think it was a bit of a trend with Labor women. Her attitude validated what I felt in my heart: it just wasn't relevant. I'd never understood the moralising in politics about what anybody did in their spare time. I wanted to be my full self, not an edited version of the truth.

The show started airing two weeks into the new job. Nine months after Glenn and I'd first met. Glenn's episodes came first; I wouldn't arrive until episode four. We watched the premiere on his laptop, on our bed, with a partially assembled cheeseboard, opting for Bega Stringers instead of Maggie Beer.

We'd watch every episode twice—once on NSW time, after I'd managed to hack 10Play to think I was over east, and again three hours later in sync with the rest of our state. I introduced Glenn to my post-show rituals, reading out what Bobette, DirtyStreetPie and GuardianAngel thought after every episode. Everything was tracking well. I was a little bit sensitive while watching early scenes of him and Helena interacting, but like in *Paradise* itself, I felt incredibly secure in our connection. I felt like we'd done the work and now we were reaping the rewards.

On the night our first date went to air, we invited over a bunch of people and had the best time. We laughed at me calling him Greg, cackled at the sexy music scoring our body-butter date and ended up in stitches at the slow-mo shots of oil being poured over my chest.

About halfway through the series, I received a message from one of my former *Bachelor in Paradise* castmates, Bill Goldsmith. The same Bill who had caused our payments to be split. While he'd ended the show with Alex Nation, they'd broken up by the time we got to the reunion. He was not portrayed in a favourable light on the show itself and he really struggled with it afterwards. He didn't return to shoot the reunion and Warner Brothers organised a cardboard cut-out in his stead.

I really liked Bill when we had originally met, in fact I always thought it was a relationship that was a bit one-sided. I think I liked him a little bit more than he liked me. He was charismatic, charming and I had wanted him to think I was cool. Things got complicated during the pandemic though—we had very different views on vaccination. I'd gone back and forth with him on some of his anti-vaccination Instagram posts about it and he'd taken it very personally.

So I was surprised to receive such an upbeat text from him. *'Alicia you big superstar. I heard you are still madly in love! Just wanted to shoot you a text to say I'm happy for ya! X.'*

I didn't reply. He'd sent me messages speculating about the outcome of the show before and the previous ones hadn't been this nice.

When I didn't reply, he messaged again six hours later—this time, with a different tone. *'Also can't believe you fucked Scot to get back at Glen for kissing Helena! That's fucken schoolyard shit! Can't wait for that to come out.'*

Not long after this, I got a tip-off that he'd spoken to a podcast called *So Dramatic!* about what had happened between Glenn and me. The podcast was dedicated to reality TV gossip. It traded in salacious stories and tell-alls. It wasn't that I believed what had happened wouldn't come out eventually, or that I wasn't prepared to speak publicly about it, I just don't think I was prepared for how actively particular people would be relishing our downfall.

I didn't know how to handle it. I felt incredibly protective of our relationship. I didn't want Glenn to look like a bad person, I didn't want to look like a bad person, and above all else I wanted people to know that we were in love. Over the final weeks of the show, a time when I should've been my happiest, I was gripped by anxiety. I spent my workdays strategising how to negotiate us out of what I thought was a terrible situation.

Midway through a workday, I messaged Glenn my latest plan. I thought we should sit on our living room couch, set up a ring light and speak very honestly about what had happened. Sort of in the realm of a YouTube apology. Take accountability for our actions, show remorse and be transparent. We'd upload it the day after the finale went to air. We could spell absolutely everything out and then we'd control the narrative. I thought it was a great idea.

Glenn very kindly disagreed. He thought it was way too much. We knew how we felt about each other and that was all that mattered. It was something that we'd navigated nine months ago and there was no need to go into granular detail with the general public.

An hour later, I received a call from the Channel Ten publicist to check how I was doing. I repeated my plan. She also kindly told me she thought it was a little over the top.

With two against one, I moved on to other ideas. Maybe a Notes App apology? Maybe I'd message *So Dramatic!* themselves and ask for a right of reply. I was deep down the rabbit hole. Glenn remained a pillar of reason and calm against my irrationality.

I was on the bus to work when the first *So Dramatic!* episode discussing the situation dropped. It was titled 'Trouble in Paradise?' I couldn't open my podcast app fast enough. The podcast host, Megan Pustetto, started by saying she hated to be the bearer of bad news but 'she has some shocking tea about our golden couple Glenn and Alisha'. My head spun as the podcast host referred to something that had caused us so much pain and heartache as 'shocking tea'.

She went on to detail what had happened and while some of her details didn't quite match ours, her treatment of it was much kinder than I had expected. Even so, in a minute and a half, *So Dramatic!* had put what had lain so heavy on my heart out into the world for everyone to feast on. As I stepped off the bus, my phone pinged with a Google alert for my name. *Daily Mail* had announced our 'shock scandal'.

I checked the comments.

'She's no looker is she—the beak on her.'

'They are all chasing the fame dragon with no sincere intentions of finding love.'

'15 minutes almost up.'

This conjecture continued until the show's grand finale. We watched it go to air on the couch of our living room, surrounded by the friends that we'd accumulated since I'd moved to Perth. Glenn's friends from high school, my friends from politics and all the others we'd made in between. Brooke was in the corner, leaning up against a bar stool where another of our friends, Jarrad, sneakily filmed our entire reaction to our commitment ceremony as it played out on screen. Then there was Gilly, one of Meg's promised men, who had since become a close friend. He was wearing a white T-shirt printed with our faces and the words 'Team Greg and Alisha'.

Glenn and I were sitting on our couch, where on any other night we'd be watching the cricket, *RuPaul's Drag Race* or whatever was on ABC. Glenn's arm was wrapped around me and his other hand was interlaced with mine on his leg. I softly squeezed his hand as we said 'I love you' on screen. The credits rolled and it was over. The final chapter on my *Bachelor* journey, closed.

But as our guests chatted and celebrated, I ducked into our bedroom. I'd spent months working on a little compilation video of all the memories we'd created together since the show. There was our time in Darwin, Glenn in Bali, trips to Dunsborough and our gnomes at Gnomesville. There were Zoom dates in the early days of Covid, my move to Perth and gardening and cooking during lockdowns. I had been editing the clips together, playing with the length of some, deleting others, figuring out which fit best with the peaks and valleys of the song in the background, 'Paradise' by Coldplay.

When I'd told Glenn about my choice of song I presented it like I'd cracked some sort of code. I was so excited to finally upload it. Against the tide of podcast episodes, *Daily Mail* articles and other commentary, I felt my video was empirical evidence that we loved each other. I'd watched endless couples finish the franchise and witnessed the subsequent speculation in group chats about whether their relationship was real or not. I wanted to show the world that we were real.

I pressed upload and watched the little, blue loading line send it out into the universe. But when I refreshed my page, the video wasn't there. Instead, there was an alert in my notifications: it was a copyright violation, I couldn't use 'Paradise' by Coldplay.

I started to panic. I'd been mapping this out for months and even at the best of times I couldn't handle it when something didn't go entirely to plan. I hid in our bedroom for a full fifteen minutes as the party continued, trying to troubleshoot the problem, Glenn came in to find me in a whirlwind, followed by our friend Mason, who looked like he immediately regretted it when he saw the state I was in. They attempted to talk me down.

'You'll get to upload it, Lish. It'll happen,' Glenn assured me.

'Just upload it tomorrow,' Mason said.

But I was in full frantic mode. The video had to go up tonight, otherwise how would people know that I loved Glenn and Glenn loved me? Mason searched for bootleg versions of the Coldplay song. I started frantically listening to random acoustic covers on YouTube. When I found one I thought could work I jammed it on top of the video and tried to upload it again. This time it worked. The first few melodic bars filled the room. I apologised for my state and I collapsed on the bed, content and relieved. It was just a little part of the experience I felt I could control. I couldn't *not* control it.

In the days following the finale, our friends supported us in force. Neil posted previously unseen pictures of us in matching ugly sweaters from Christmas in July celebrations that had passed in secret, our Darwin friends posted photos of us partying at Throb that we'd carefully omitted Glenn from at the time. And everyone who had come over to watch the last episode posted pictures that we'd taken, celebrating our final chapter.

Other people were less complimentary. Bill, clearly unsatisfied that I wasn't being completely demolished by both the media and the audience, took to his Instagram stories to share one of the *Daily Mail*'s articles that framed our transgressions as 'hook-ups', with the caption 'Wait until you hear the full details hahahaha' alongside the squirting water emoji and the eggplant emoji. He finished it off with a hashtag: #SheWasThirsty.

Bill wasn't our only detractor. Whenever I came across negative comments, I'd fixate on them.

'Do these people have any morals?'

'If it were me I would not take him back.'

'She's an idiot.'

The majority of the reception had been positive, supportive and nuanced. But I couldn't see it. I was blinded by the bad.

Conclusion

I was back in the power of other people's opinions, as though I had never been any other way. At any one time my happiness was determined by someone with the username ShelleyinAus or Barry75.

Glenn could feel it. In the days since the finale, he had watched me struggle. He could sense my mood shift when I read a thread with the pronouncement 'Once a cheater, always a cheater' or when I'd stumble upon a Facebook comment that said we wouldn't last beyond the end of the month. I knew what Glenn and I had was real, but I was allowing these strangers to define my reality.

I could see the pattern and knew my response needed to change. But it was so incredibly difficult: I cared so much and I couldn't stop. It was how I'd always been, with everything and everyone.

It was the casting directors reading my *Bachelor* application. I'd shaped and reshaped that application to try to appear to be someone I thought they would consider worthwhile.

It was how I'd operated in the Labor Party, constantly afraid that if I was just a little too *myself*, or had an opinion that didn't completely align with the collective, I'd be rejected. I wouldn't have a place, I wouldn't be promoted and I couldn't do the work I so desperately wanted to do. Some of those fears were legitimate—there are circumstances in which politics can be really cruel, sexist and suffocating—but some of it I constructed and used to compound the narrative that I was unworthy, unintelligent or unwanted.

It was how I'd acted with the producers on the show. When they'd ask me a question, I'd deliver the exact answer I thought they were looking for. When I'd felt I wasn't delivering, or wasn't being exciting or dramatic enough, I'd extend myself, pushing the boundaries of my own comfort just to be compliant. The sound of their laughter after a bitchy comment or mean observation became fuel to my fire. I'd be meaner, nastier, more cutting, in search of their approval.

It was how I interacted with men—with 'The One' and with Jules. I handed over my sense of self-worth to them to judge and determine. Every date was a dance around whether they liked me or not, whether I was good enough for them. I'd rarely stop to think about whether I liked them or whether they were good enough for me.

It was what I'd done with Bobette too. I'd hung on her every word, her every post, for almost five years. I'd typed the same letters into my search bar every day, refreshing minute by minute to see if her appraisal of me had changed. I didn't even know if she was a 'she'. I didn't know who Bobette was at all.

For so much of my life I'd felt like I was trying to solve a problem. I would read books, scroll websites, go to therapy and listen to podcasts, trying to reach some sort of conclusive answer. My mind was always busy, sifting through conflicting thoughts, trying to figure out what I believed, what was right, what was wrong, what was good and what was bad. Constantly trying to figure out who I was, where I fit in and whether I was doing a good job. I wanted confirmation. I wanted validation. But there was always a void, a compartment I couldn't manage to fill—a personality paradox, someone I couldn't get on board, a situation that remained shades of grey, rather than black and white.

Life isn't like the reality TV shows I'd been consuming since I could comprehend them. It doesn't have a clear beginning, middle and end. There are no convenient narrative structures, no easily defined characters and the stories in my own life aren't resolved in a neat ninety minutes. They are messy, nuanced and ever-evolving.

I tried to reflect on the times I thought I'd been doing well. When I thought I'd been doing a good job. When I thought I'd been a good person. The operative word in all of those sentences being 'I'. For me, making and trusting my own decisions around the 'cheating scandal' and making and trusting my own decision to move to Perth were huge moments of personal growth. I came to realise that every time I trusted my own thoughts and feelings, magic happened.

I reflected on other times I'd just gone with my gut. Finally cutting it off with The One, deciding to go on *The Bachelor* in the first place, leaving NSW Labor when it became toxic. I started to reframe all these big decisions and hard things into beacons, showing me when I had been doing my best work. For way too long, I had been outsourcing my own decision-making. I'd been outsourcing my own happiness.

There was always going to be someone who did not value my work or someone who didn't believe in my relationship. There was always going to be someone who thought I was annoying, unattractive, undeserving. I needed to stop trying to find a solution to their doubts and a pretty bow to tie it all together neatly.

Glenn and I did make it beyond that month. We made it beyond the predictions of many of the comments I'd taken so vehemently to heart. Glenn proposed on my birthday, nearly two years after we'd met, on the South Perth Foreshore, one of his favourite places. Now one of mine. No cameras, no audio, no surveillance, just us. We rang my mum first, then Hannah. Then we drank a bottle of very expensive champagne and ate two dozen oysters at a restaurant he'd booked for us to celebrate. I uploaded a selfie we'd taken on the jetty where he'd proposed the next day.

I couldn't help but check the forum a couple of hours later.

Bobette had shared the news: 'Sincere congratulations to Alisha and Glenn; my favourite forum lurkers.'

I flicked through the reactions from the other forum regulars.

'They always felt solid to me, despite some initial drama.'

'Congratulations to the happy couple.'

I closed the tab and locked my phone. I was happy they were happy, but, more importantly, I was happy. I didn't need a ring, a rose or a comment for confirmation.

Acknowledgements

Writing *The Villain Edit* has been both the biggest challenge and biggest joy. It wouldn't exist without the help of so many. Firstly, to Tessa, my commissioning editor at Allen & Unwin, thanks for sitting with me at a Rozelle coffee shop and letting me wax lyrical for hours as we talked through what this book could be. I can't thank you enough for your support throughout the writing journey—I enjoyed my many therapy sessions over Zoom. To the rest of the Allen & Unwin team, particularly Aziza and Angela, thank you for sharpening my language and shaping my words.

To Glenn, thank you for being my most incredible support. Thank you for listening to me rattle off paragraphs to you every day for months, for believing in me when I'm not the best at it and for being open to sharing our rawest moments in the hopes they might help someone else feel less alone.

To Hannah, James, Dylan, Zak and Elliott, who were the first to read what I'd put together and provided such valuable feedback, I appreciate you all so much. A special shout-out to the group chat for always being available to help me find an elusive word.

Thank you to everyone who has been a feature of my story so far. To my fellow staffers, former bosses (good and bad), stupol comrades and my Bachelor family—particularly Alex, Cat, Romy, the Warner Brothers and Channel Ten production teams, fans of the franchise and Bobette—without you, there wouldn't be me.

And finally, thanks to you, for allowing me to share my fullest self with you through this book. I'm very grateful that you picked it up. I hope you enjoyed the journey.